NIETZSCHE'S COMING GOD
or The Redemption of the Divine

Originally published in French in 2005 by Editions Connaissances et Savoirs, Paris, under the title: *Le Dieu à venir de Nietzsche, ou la rédemption du divin.*

First English edition published in 2013 by Arktos Media Ltd.

ISBN 978-1-907166-90-7

BIC classification:
Social & political philosophy (HPS)

Translation: Abir Taha
Proofreader: Tobias Ridderstråle
Cover Design: Andreas Nilsson and Daniel Friberg
Layout: Daniel Friberg

ARKTOS MEDIA LTD
www.arktos.com

NIETZSCHE'S COMING GOD

or *The Redemption of the Divine*

Abir Taha

ARKTOS
London, 2013

To Friedrich Nietzsche,
the greatest mind and richest soul

Table of Contents

"O Zarathustra, with such disbelief you are more pious than you believe.
Some god in you has converted you to your godlessness."
— *Thus Spoke Zarathustra*

INTRODUCTION

The Real Nietzsche

F riedrich Nietzsche is generally viewed as the absolute nihilist, the ultimate atheist, the "Antichrist," the "murderer" of God, the immoral iconoclast whose "philosophy with a hammer" broke the idols of Judeo-Christianity: "God," "Morality," "Truth," etc. In fact, to Nietzsche, these Christian ideals were nothing but "false truths," lies and illusions whose transcendental nature led to the negation of life and consequently to nihilism, rendering the death of *this* god necessary and even desirable. In this sense, Nietzsche is the philosopher who dared to push nihilism to its extreme limits.

However, to retain from Nietzschean thought merely its nihilistic, pessimistic, destructive aspect, even if it is a characteristic and essential—albeit incomplete—aspect of that philosophy, would be to understand it only partially and to fail to grasp its real motivation and creative and spiritual dimension which goes well beyond a mere refutation and systematic destruction of false beliefs. Indeed, Nietzsche's spirituality, his creative—even mystical—side, has long and often been ignored, along with the fact that to him, nihilism—which was undeniably an inherent and essential part of his philosophy—was nonetheless not an *end* in itself (as it is—alas!—generally considered nowadays), but a transitory phase that he used in order to achieve his task of destruction of the false Judeo-Christian ideals (which he nevertheless contrasted with Christ's original message) and his "transvaluation", or revaluation,of all values.

Nietzsche's nihilism was a necessary but transitory phase which was meant to precede his grand and veritable task of reconstruction, of creation: the *Übermensch*, the Superman, who embodies the advanced stage of a superior humanity which would have transcended its "human, all-too-human" nature, to reach a supra-human, post-human stage, in conformity with the Nietzschean vital principle of eternal becoming and self-overcoming.

This book thus aims to show how Nietzsche, who augured and lived nihilism in its profoundest depths, nonetheless ended up defeating it — after having used it as a "hammer" to destroy the old law-tables — by overcoming and transcending it; that is, by turning the death of God, which is at the same time the consequence and culmination of nihilism, into an act of liberation of man — the liberation from old beliefs, namely the millenarian "lies" of Judeo-Christianity which have enslaved the human spirit and have prevented man's spiritual progress and evolution.

To Nietzsche, the death of God therefore became an "active nihilism," creator of new values, in other words a nihilism that had "defeated itself," or "accomplished nihilism." Nietzsche could thus be described as an "anti-nihilist nihilist," the philosopher who had predicted, acknowledged and experienced nihilism, using it against itself in order to destroy it by transcending it, thereby turning the calamity of the death of God into a prelude to the rebirth of the divine and to man's elevation and self-overcoming.

By analysing the cause, the significance, and the consequence of the "death of God" declared by Nietzsche, I will endeavour to demonstrate that nihilism, as prophesied by the German philosopher, represented to him — in the final analysis –merely a necessary dose of "immoralism" to realise a total transvaluation of values. I will argue that Nietzsche's nihilism was only a transitory stage, a "moment," and had a destructive role to play which would nonetheless end as soon as it was accomplished, thus paving the way for Nietzsche's final and decisive phase, his true goal: the creation of the Superman, the man who has overcome himself, the incarnation of the coming god, the immanent and accessible god, in contrast to the old, false god of monotheism, transcendent to life, unreachable, and thus life-negating.

According to Nietzsche, the will to power is the *Lebensphilosophie* (the "philosophy of life"), the vital creative concept "beyond good and evil" which, by affirming and blessing life and its law of eternal overcoming, would transcend and overcome the life-denying Christian morality, and would thereby save the world from nihilism — which is at the same time the cause and the consequence of the death of God — thus offering lost humanity a new hope, a new promise of noontide and eternity, a new supreme goal: the Superman.

I will then expound what I have termed Nietzsche's "spiritual atheism," a brand of atheism which is unique in the fact that it does not stop at the death of God (and therefore cannot be confused with it), for

Nietzsche considered that the death of God was not an end but merely the death of *a* god, the god of "monotono-theism," as he liked to describe it.

I will show how, after having perceived, recognised and celebrated the "death of God," Nietzsche overcame the divine death, not only by making it a great liberation for the enlightened, higher man, but also by refusing to sink into an absolute atheism which would also deny life by wresting a higher end away from it, thereby leading to a second nihilism, the nihilism of "egalitarian" and "decadent" modernity, the nihilism of the "last men" with their dull "realism" and vulgar and hedonistic virtues. I argue that, in the final analysis, Nietzsche's spiritual atheism was merely a prelude to a spiritual rebirth, to the advent of the Superman as the incarnation of the new mode of divinity.

Thus, the death of God for Nietzsche is only a "moment" in evolution and in history, and not a fatal end, given that it is only the death of *a* god, *not* the divine. Consequently, and conversely, it is a new beginning, a new dawn for a higher, *post-modern* humanity (modernity incarnating, according to Nietzsche, nihilism and decadence), a higher humanity which, in its search for perfection and eternal overcoming, would reject both the religious obscurantist dogma as well as the Cartesian rationalist dogma.

Nietzsche was *not* the absolute nihilist and atheist materialist as he is — alas! — perceived nowadays. If he himself admitted that he was *the* godless (*Gottlos*) man par excellence, he was nonetheless not an atheist in the ordinary sense of the word, but in a much deeper and more spiritual sense: he was *pagan*, a pagan pantheist, a disciple of Dionysus and Manu, venerating the ancient cult of the God-Man, of the *Naturreligion* — the "Religion of Nature" — or what he termed "the Dionysian festive procession from India to Greece." The Superman, the Nietzschean dream of "Noontide and Eternity," thus reveals himself in Dionysus, who incarnates the redemption of the divine, Nietzsche's "coming god."

CHAPTER ONE

The Death of God, or the "End of the Longest Error"

-I- Symptom of decadence: The death of God as the outcome and culmination of nihilism

"God is dead": by issuing this famous philosophical sentence, probably the most meaningful statement in the history of human thought, Nietzsche announces the *Götzen-Dämmerung*, the "twilight of the idols" of Judeo-Christianity: religion, morality, God, truth, and other similar concepts. He then proceeds in his many writings to analyse the sombre reasons that have led to this divine death, namely the nihilism resulting from the belief in this old god, this false god that humanity has venerated for millennia.

For Nietzsche, God is indeed dead, and, along with him, religion and all old, false beliefs and superstitions, more specifically the transcendental, anti-natural and life-denying Judeo-Christian monotheism. In his book *The Gay Science,* the German philosopher makes this grave statement: "What are these churches now, if they are not the tombs and monuments of God?"[1]

It is worth noting, however, that Nietzsche himself is *not* the murderer of God. He only *perceives* this death. God is already dead, but mankind has yet to realise that. Nietzsche is thus the herald who *announces* God's death to the world. That is the task that Nietzsche had taken upon himself to achieve.

Yet one can only wonder: what was it that led to the death of God? In other words, *why* did God die? Or rather, *which* god is dead? By "God," Nietzsche means the god of transcendental monotheism and Christian

---

1   Friedrich Nietzsche, *Le Gai Savoir* (*The Gay Science*) (Paris: Editions Gallimard, 1950), p. 168.

morality, whom he contrasts with the divine (we shall see that in the third chapter which deals with Nietzsche's "spiritual atheism").We shall see later that Nietzsche had his own pantheistic, pagan vision of divinity. Therefore, it is the "God" of Judeo-Christianity who is dead, but the divine is something totally different to Nietzsche; it is immanent in nature and in man.

God is dead because he denied life, he was above and beyond life. It is the belief in *this* transcendent—and hence unreachable—god which has led to nihilism, for man, by denying this life as false and meaningless, and by venerating an imaginary beyond or afterlife as "the real world," has ended up negating life and negating himself. In *The Will to Power*, Nietzsche writes:

> We are starting to discern the contrast between the world that we are venerating and the world that we are experiencing, the world that we are. A choice is left for us: to destroy either our veneration, or ourselves. In the latter case, it is nihilism.[2]

He continues:

> A nihilist is a man who judges that the world as it is should not exist, and the world as it should be does not exist. Therefore, to live (to act, to suffer, to will, to feel) makes no sense: that which is pathetic in nihilism is to know that "all is vain."[3]

It was mankind itself which, through its obsession of an afterlife promised by the god of monotheism, ended up denying the real world to realise afterwards that the imaginary world does not exist. Nietzsche explains how the (so-called) "real world" became a myth—or what he calls the "history of an error" —concluding that "with the real world, we have also abolished the apparent world!"[4]

Nihilism has thus become irreversible; the death of God is its apex and its logical consequence. Belief in an unknown, unreachable "God," a "Kingdom of Heaven" beyond earthly life, has led to the nihilism which characterises modernity.

---

2   Friedrich Nietzsche, *La Volonté de Puissance* (*The Will to Power*) (Paris: Gallimard, 1995), vol. II, p. 9.

3   Ibid., p.11.

4   Friedrich Nietzsche, *Crépuscule des Idoles* (*Twilight of the idols*) (Paris: Gallimard, 1974), pp. 30-31.

Nietzsche makes this prophecy when he declares in *The Will to Power*: "what I am recounting is the history of the two coming centuries. I am describing what will come, what cannot fail to come: the advent of nihilism."[5]

-II- The roots of nihilism: Christian life-denying morality

Christianity: An anti-natural religion hostile to life

Nietzsche's Zarathustra, by making his sombre existential statement announcing God's demise, is thereby prophesising the "twilight of the idols," the decline of Christian morality which, by inventing a "beyond" and promising a better life after death, and by attributing perfection solely to this "hidden world"—whilst condemning the real world as imperfect and tainted with sin—has led to the depreciation of life, maintaining man for millennia under the mental and moral yoke of an abstract, distant, unreachable "God," thus preventing him from pursuing his highest goal, the only accessible goal in life, which is none other than self-perfection and self-overcoming.

It is the hope of finding salvation and perfection in the "other," *post-mortem* world that has incited men to accept and bear their imperfections and their weaknesses in *this* world; consequently, instead of striving to become perfect—or at least to improve themselves—in the real world, they put all their hopes in a distant and undefined future: "Suffering and weakness... that is what created all afterworlds."[6] Nietzsche elaborates:

> The notion of "God," invented as an antithesis to life—as all that is harmful, poisoned, negating, all the mortal hatred against life, all that brought back to a scandalous unity! The notion of "afterlife," of the "real world," invented for the sole purpose of depreciating the only world that exists, of not keeping any goal, any task for our terrestrial reality! The notion of "soul," "spirit," and, finally, of "immortal soul," invented for the sole purpose of despising the body, of making it sick—"holy"![7]

---

5   Friedrich Nietzsche, *The Will to Power*, vol. II, p. 23.

6   Friedrich Nietzsche, *Ainsi Parlait Zarathoustra* (*Thus Spoke Zarathustra*) (Paris: Gallimard, 1971), p. 42.

7   Friedrich Nietzsche, *Ecce Homo* (Paris: Gallimard, 1974), p. 195.

Thus, it is the transcendental character of Christian morality that has led to the negation of life, for that morality placed its highest ideals — God, Truth, the Good, Salvation, and so on — above and beyond life itself life. In this sense, Christian morality is anti-natural, for nature is beyond good and evil (the weak man having invented morality to protect himself against the strong). The nihilism resulting from morality therefore found its culmination in the death of the lie called "God," given that this morality was nothing but a pure and simple negation of truth — in the name of so-called "eternal truth" and the "real world" — and hence a devaluation of life; consequently, Nietzsche considers that Christianity was:

> From the start, essentially and radically, satiety and disgust with life which hide and disguise themselves only under the semblance of faith in "another" life, a "better" life. The hatred for the "world," the anathema towards passions, the fear of beauty and pleasure, a beyond invented in order to better denigrate the present, essentially a desire of nothingness, of death, of rest, until the "Sabbath of Sabbaths" — all this, as well as Christianity's absolute pretention to take only moral values into account seemed to me the most dangerous, the most worrying form of a "will to annihilation," or at least the sign of a deep weakening, lassitude, discouragement, exhaustion, impoverishment of life — for, in the name of morality (particularly Christian, that is, absolute morality), life must always and inexorably be at fault, for life is something that is essentially immoral — and life, finally stifled under the weight of contempt and eternal negation, must be felt as unworthy of being desired and as a non-value in itself. Morality itself — could it be that morality itself is a "will to negate life," a secret instinct of annihilation, a principle of ruin, of deterioration, of denigration, the beginning of the end? And, consequently, the danger of dangers?[8]

To Nietzsche, it is the Christian belief in a transcendent god and in an afterlife, as well as the notion of the equality of all souls before this moral and transcendent — and hence unreachable — god, which has pushed man to escape the harsh earthly reality in order to find refuge in the sweet illusion of "another" world, the sole hope for a better life for the weak, the failures, and all those who suffer from life as an unbearable burden.

---

8   Friedrich Nietzsche, *La Naissance de la Tragédie* (*The Birth of Tragedy*) (Paris: Librairie Générale française, 1994), pp. 40-41.

As a result, Nietzsche rejected and despised Christianity as an "anti-Aryan religion par excellence" (as he writes in *Antichrist*), in the sense of it being an anti-pagan and anti-ancient (and more particularly anti-Greek and anti-Hindu) religion which denies life by preaching and venerating a "real world" hidden in the skies, a religion which represents the antithesis to the tragic and ancient spirit which affirms life and blesses it as it is, in all its innocence and cruelty.

Christianity is thus an anti-natural religion, for it is monotheistic, transcendental, and moral, instead of being polytheistic, immanent, beyond good and evil, as were the natural religions of antiquity, from Brahmanic India to Dionysian Greece. It was hence natural for Nietzsche, the pagan, the Greek, to contrast the pagan spirit with the Christian spirit embodied respectively and perfectly by Dionysus—who represents "the religious affirmation of life"—and by the "innocent Crucified," the apex of suffering and weakness. "Dionysus versus the Crucified": the pagan versus the Christian vision of the world. That was Nietzsche's epic "war of the spirits" which characterises the history of human thought and encapsulates the Aryan-Semitic eternal spiritual conflict.

Paul's Judeo-Christian "Dysangel": A betrayal of Christ's original message

It is worth noting that when Nietzsche contrasts Dionysus with the "Crucified," he is thereby rejecting the image of the "innocent victim" presented by the Church in order to subjugate the masses by focusing on Christ's crucifixion, his humiliating death, instead of extolling his exemplary life which Nietzsche saw as a model for mankind to follow.

It is in this sense that Nietzsche proclaimed himself the "Antichrist," that is, the anti-Crucified. Therefore, and despite the fact that Nietzsche denounced Christianity as a life-denying religion, he nonetheless distinguished it from, and contrasted it with, Christ's life and practice, considering that it was the disciples of Jesus, particularly Paul, who had distorted what Nietzsche calls "Primitive Christianity," i.e. Christ's original teachings and message, turning them into a religion "for the sick and the meek," a religion which denies reality and life and has thereby systematically destroyed all the natural, healthy, superior values of the ancient tradition from India to Greece: "Christianity has robbed us of the entire harvest of ancient culture,"[9] Nietzsche writes, crying out with indignation "all the work of the ancient world... utterly in vain!"[10]

Indeed, to Nietzsche, "'Christianity' is something very different from what its founder has done and intended. It is the great anti-pagan movement of antiquity... it is the advent of pessimism... and of the pessimism of the weak, the vanquished, the suffering, the oppressed. The Christians have as mortal enemies: strength of character, spirit, and taste... they have as mortal enemies the Romans as well as the Greeks."[11]

Christianity thus represents the religion of the herd, the masses, the oppressed, the slaves, and all those who suffer from life as a burden and a curse and view death as a liberation; it is hence the sworn enemy of classical ideals and of the noble religion of pagan and tragic antiquity which affirms and blesses life in its totality, accepting its cruelty and its immoralism.

Nonetheless, this "decadent" religion is, according to Nietzsche, nothing but a grotesque distortion of Christ's original vision and message, a religion which has "waged a fight to the death against this superior type of humanity... Christianity has taken the side of all that is base, lowly, failed, it has made an ideal of the opposition to the instinct of preservation of strong life."[12]

Because of this, Christianity has been "the greatest tragedy that mankind has known until the present."[13] The Church is "exactly that against which Jesus has preached, and that against which he has taught his disciples to fight."[14] Consequently, Nietzsche considered that Christianity and its instrument of power, the Church (which embodies the will to power of the priests), were the perfect antithesis of the Evangel, of the spirit and the practice of Jesus. He believed that "the greatest irony in universal history" lay in the fact that "mankind was on its knees before the exact opposite of what was the origin, the meaning, the *raison d'être* of the Evangel."[15] "Christianity" thus rhymes perfectly with "nihilism."[16]

9   Friedrich Nietzsche, *L'Antéchrist (Antichrist)* (Paris: Gallimard, 1974), p. 85.
10 Ibid., p. 83.
11 Friedrich Nietzsche, *The Will to Power*, vol. I, p. 189.
12 Friedrich Nietzsche, *Antichrist*, p. 17.
13 Ibid., p. 70.
14 Friedrich Nietzsche, *The Will to Power*, vol. I, p. 203.
15 Friedrich Nietzsche, *Antichrist*, p. 50.
16 Ibid., p. 83.

Thus, Nietzsche believed that Christianity, which represents the degeneration of the vital values and virtues of Hindus and Greeks, was unworthy of its founder Jesus, whom he perceived as a free spirit preaching the mystical doctrine of the "Kingdom of Heaven in us." Indeed, Nietzsche saw in Jesus a rebel against the Pharisees, against the Jewish priests' dogmatic and narrow spirit, those same priests who, through Paul, have deformed Christ's life-affirming doctrine which was destined for free and higher spirits. According to Nietzsche, that doctrine was totally distorted by Paul, who transformed it into a rigid, ritualistic, superstitious and transcendental dogma aimed at rendering life more bearable to life's unfruitful and unworthy failures.

For Nietzsche, Jesus was the sole and last Christian[17] who preached "primitive Christianity," a mystical doctrine whose immanent—and hence natural—notion of the "Kingdom of God within us," which affirms life and elevates man, was totally antithetical to the image of the transcendental, anthropomorphic and jealous god-judge of Judeo-Christian monotheism. Jesus' Christianity—in contrast to Paul's Judeo-Christianity—was, in the eyes of Nietzsche, "a practice, and not a doctrine. He tells us how to act, not what to believe."[18] Consequently, this original Christianity "will always be possible in any epoch,"[19] given that it is linked to no dogma, that it is supra-historical and universal.

Nietzsche condemned Judeo-Christianity principally because it had deliberately misinterpreted and distorted Christ's original message, which incarnated the principle of the mystical union between Man and God, the immanent god, that is, the spiritual, interior, supra-historical doctrine of primitive Christianity, in contrast to Paul's historical and dogmatic doctrine and its notion of the "Kingdom of Heaven in the beyond," namely its belief in a transcendental and unreachable "God." The following passage from the *Antichrist* shows Nietzsche's respect for Jesus: "Jesus had yet abolished the idea of 'fault,' he had denied any gap between man and God: he had lived the 'God-man' unity, and he had lived it as his 'Glad Tidings' and not as a privilege."[20]

It was Christ's disciples, these "lost souls," who had turned him into a Pharisee and a theologian, and, in their frenetic veneration, "they could

17 "In truth, there has only been one Christian, and he died on the cross." Ibid., p. 52.
18 Friedrich Nietzsche, *The Will to Power*, vol. I, p 178.
19 Friedrich Nietzsche, *Antichrist*, p.52.
20 Ibid., p. 55.

no longer admit this general 'equality' taught by Jesus, which allows each one to say he is the Son of God: their revenge consisted in exalting Jesus in an extravagant manner, to distance him from them, just as they did, in the past, to take their revenge on their enemies—the Jews had severed their God from themselves and had put him 'in the clouds'... the unique God and the Unique Son of God: both born of resentment."[21]

Nietzsche believed that Christianity was possible as a practice, as a private way of life, but not as a belief, a rigid dogma. He considered that "all the orthodox Christian doctrine, all the so-called Christian 'truth' is but an illusion and a lie, and the absolute opposite of what gave the impulse to the Christian movement. What is Christian in the ecclesiastic sense is in essence *anti-Christian*: things and persons replacing symbols; stories instead of eternal facts; formulas, rites, dogmas, instead of a way of life. Real Christianity would consist in the total indifference to dogmas, to prayer, to priests, to the Church, to theology."[22]

Contrary to the Church's doctrine which is attached to rites and dogmas, Jesus "addresses himself directly to the interior reality," to "the Kingdom of Heaven which is in the heart; he doesn't believe in the efficiency of Jewish orthodox observance; he doesn't even take into account the reality of Judaism... he is purely interior." Also, this "great symbolist," Jesus, "does not attach himself to the crude formulas which regulate the commerce with God; he defends himself against the whole doctrine of expiation and redemption; he shows how one should live in order to feel united with God—and how one cannot do that by penitence and contrition regarding the subject of one's sins; sin 'is without importance,' that is his principal judgement... the Kingdom of Heaven is a state of the heart... it is not 'above the earth.' The Kingdom of God 'comes' not historically or chronologically, according to the calendar, as a thing would come a certain day and not on the eve; yet it is a 'change of heart in the individual,' a thing that comes at all times and is however never here."[23]

Indeed, Nietzsche thought that nothing is more anti-Christian than the ecclesiastical platitudes of a personal god, of a "Kingdom of God" in the beyond, of a "Son of God," arguing that the "Kingdom of God" is not "something we await" but rather an inner experience which Jesus sought to share with the world, for original Christianity needs "neither

21 Ibid.
22 Friedrich Nietzsche, *The Will to Power*, vol. I, p. 204.
23 Ibid., pp. 174-175.

a personal God, nor sin, nor immortality, nor redemption, nor faith,"[24] given that it is a practice, a way of living in inner peace, and not a dogma. It was the Church's distortion of Christ's original message (in order to enslave the masses by imposing the "virtues" of submission and humility on them) which, by transforming this inner state of mind and experience into a "Kingdom of God in Heaven," heralded the break between Christianity and Christ's original teaching. Thus spoke Nietzsche: "The very word *Christianity* is based on a misunderstanding: in truth, there has only been one Christian, and he died on the cross. The 'Evangel' died on the cross. From this moment on, what we call 'Evangel' is already the opposite of what Jesus himself had lived: 'bad tidings,' a 'Dysangel.'"[25]

Therefore, primitive Christianity represented to Nietzsche (as it does to the Christian mystics) an inner experience, a practice, and not an outer, abstract "truth." Consequently, real Christianity in no way implies blind adherence to a limited number of fixed ideas ("God," the "Afterlife," or "heaven"), but is rather a direct spiritual experience with the mystics' "inner God" or "God within." It is this fundamental difference which distinguishes Aryan pagan spirituality from Semitic monotheistic religiosity, the former rejecting any gulf between this world and the other, between Man and God (the Nietzschean cult of the Superman precisely aims to fill this gulf between the human and the divine). Indeed, the natural, pagan religion considers that divinity is immanent in nature and in life.

This immanence which characterises Christ's initial message was completely distorted and perverted by Paul, the second Judas who, according to Nietzsche, betrayed Jesus by transforming the true monistic, pantheistic, supra-historical, and spiritual messageof primitive Christianity (or rather of "Christism"), into a monotheistic, transcendental, historical, dogmatic and anthropomorphic religion (which has thus become "Judeo-Christianity"), impregnating it with the narrow and heinous spirit of the priests, which is the exact opposite of Christ's original message.

Nietzsche thus accused Christian morality of having betrayed—through Paul—Christ's original message; he condemned the egalitarian Christian "gregarious values" which lead to levelling and general mediocrity.

24 Ibid., p. 177.
25 Friedrich Nietzsche, *Antichrist*, p. 52.

According to Nietzsche, Paul, the "Dysangelist," embodied the spirit of the priests, he was the priest who was aspiring to power and hence "the type opposed to the 'bringer of glad tidings': the genius in hatred, in visionary hatred, in hatred's ruthless logic... first, the Redeemer: he nailed him to the cross. The life, example, teaching, death, sense and justification of the entire Evangel—nothing was left of it when this fraud by hatred understood what alone could serve his ends. *Not* reality, *not* historical truth."[26]

Judeo-Christianity, which is the perfect incarnation of the spirit and will to power of the priests (represented by Paul), this Jewish sacramental spirit which Jesus rejected and despised, the total opposite of primitive Christianity, Judeo-Christianity now ruled the world. That, according to Nietzsche, was the tragic irony of history. Paul had eliminated primitive Christianity by reestablishing what Jesus had annulled through his practice and his life. Therefore, Nietzsche affirmed: *"Deus, qualem Paulus creavit, dei negation"* ("God, as created by Paul, is a negation of God").[27]

Hence, to Nietzsche, the Church represents the antithesis to everything Jesus had preached and fought against... this explains why Nietzsche—alias Zarathustra –proclaimed himself *Gottlos* ("Godless"), considering that it was precisely his belief in the *real* God, the divine—and not the "God" created by Paul—which had pushed him to deny monotheism's Judeo-Christian God.

Nietzsche accused Paul of having distorted and inverted Christ's original message which was meant to liberate man from the Pharisees' rigid monotheism and to elevate him to the divine level, instead turning Christ's teachings into a monotheistic transcendental and levelling religion preaching "equality of souls before God," submission, weakness, pity, and humility, as well as the impossibility of man's perfection due to his "sinful," inferior nature.

Indeed, the spirit of Christ is immanent, monistic, an elevation of Man towards God, whereas the monotheistic Judeo-Christian spirit is transcendent, a fall from God to Man. Therefore, to Nietzsche, Christianity was but Judaism under another form, more universal, but also more hypocritical, incarnating the hatred of Jewish priests under

---

26 Ibid., p. 56.
27 Ibid., p. 64.

the form of "Christian love," a "form of liberated Judaism,"[28] a "Jewish church of Christian confession."[29]

This explains why Nietzsche despised the Christian anti-Semites of Germany, whom he considered to be mere Jews of Christian confession; the irony lay in the fact that the religion that they were using with such confidence against the Jews was but the ultimate consequence of Judaism, its continuation and not its negation (Jesus being the last Christian), as the following passage shows:

> The Jews are the most fateful of people: through their influence, they have rendered man so fake that today, a Christian can feel anti-Jewish sentiments, without understanding that he is but the ultimate consequence of Judaism.[30]

Thus, to Nietzsche, Paul's Judeo-Christianity was the product of the Jews, the ultimate and logical consequence of Judaism, and *not*—as Christian anti-Semites would like to believe—a movement opposed to the instinct of the priests. Indeed, Jesus was the only and the last Christian, and the movement, launched by Paul, which succeeded him represented this priestly spirit that Jesus so vehemently fought against. Nietzsche, the pagan life-affirmer who considered that "God" is the word which expresses the big "yes" to all things,[31] despised the Christian as much as he despised the Jew, and *precisely* because the Christian is nothing more than a Jew: "The Christian is only a Jew of a 'freer confession'... the Christian, this *ultima ratio* of lie, is the Jew once more, even thrice more."[32]

Nietzsche rejected Christianity precisely because the latter, instead of being—as Jesus wanted it—a spiritual liberating message advocating the return to the notion of the God-Man so characteristic of the natural and noble religion of antiquity, was in the final analysis only a consecration and a confirmation of monotheism, of Judaism.

---

28 Friedrich Nietzsche, *The Will to Power*, vol. I, p. 184.

29 Ibid., p. 179.

30 Friedrich Nietzsche, *Antichrist*, p. 36.

31 "Are pagan all those who say yes to life, those for whom 'God' is the word which expresses the big 'yes' to all things." Ibid., p. 76.

32 Ibid., pp. 59-60.

The genealogy of Christian morality: An inversion of natural values, or how the real world became a myth

As we have seen above, according to Nietzsche, Judeo-Christianity, whose life-denying morality preaches transcendence (the "beyond") and all sorts of "ideals" hostile to reality and to nature, has led to nihilism and to the death of God, or what Nietzsche called the "end of the longest error." In the *Antichrist*, Nietzsche condemns Christianity as the "victory of the *Chandala* values, the glad tidings preached to the humble and the poor, the general uprising of all those who are trampled upon, miserable, fake, losers, against 'race' — it is the immortal revenge of the *Chandala* presented as the religion of love."[33]

Nietzsche deplores the rule of "slave morality," the values of the weak and wretched, a rule rendered possible by Christianity whose historical universal mission was to achieve the victory of *homo vulgaris*, the monotheistic and Judeo-Christian vulgar man, over his ancient masters, pagans, Greeks, Romans, which meant the "Judaisation" and later the "Christianisation" of the world:

> Let us submit to the facts; that the people have triumphed—or the slaves, or the populace, or the herd, or whatever name you care to give them—if this happened through the Jews, so be it! In that case no nation ever had a greater mission in the world's history. The "masters" have been done away with; the morality of the vulgar man has triumphed. This triumph may also be called a blood-poisoning (it has mutually fused the races)—I do not dispute it; but there is no doubt that this intoxication has succeeded. The "redemption" of the human race (that is, from the masters) is progressing swimmingly; everything is obviously becoming Judaised, or Christianised, or vulgarised (what is there in the words?).[34]

In Nietzsche's view, world history is characterised by the eternal conflict between the vulgar, egalitarian Judeo-Christian values and the pagan aristocratic values of antiquity. Nietzsche believed that the "Judaisation" of Christianity itself (i.e. the distortion and inversion of the Gospel, of Christ's original message, or what Nietzsche approvingly calls "primitive Christianity"), and the subsequent gradual Judaisation of the

---

33 Friedrich Nietzsche, *Twilight of the idols*, p. 50.
34 Friedrich Nietzsche, *La Généalogie de la Morale* (*On the Genealogy of Morals*) (Paris: Gallimard, 1971), pp. 33-34.

world through Christianity—which embodies the resentment of the weak—was mainly the work of Paul, the priest, the "eternal Jew" par excellence, "*Chandala* hatred against Rome, against 'the world,' become flesh and genius."[35] Paul had annulled primitive Christianity by inverting all ancient values.

It is worth noting that when Nietzsche condemned the Jews, he did not do so as a conventional anti-Semite; rather, he did so as a good pagan who denounced the priestly spirit which characterises Judaism (and which later extended to the Christian world through the priest Paul). In this sense, Nietzsche, the pagan, despised the Christians just as much as he despised the Jews as incarnations of the spirit and state of mind of the priests so characteristic of monotheism, or what he calls "the priest within us," a spirit which lives on nowadays through the quasi-universal reign of Judeo-Christianity. Thus did Zarathustra deplore, "It is within us that he still dwells, the old priest of idols."[36]

Going back to the rule of *Chandala* values, we ask ourselves: how did this victory of slaves take place? And how did it lead to nihilism? To Nietzsche, the "slaves," i.e. the monotheists—Jews, then Christians—have vanquished their old (Roman) masters through the most incredible inversion produced in the history of human thought: through a "slave revolt" (imbued with the priestly spirit) in the field of morality, by converting Romans to Christianity. With the Jews, writes Nietzsche, "begins the slave revolt in morals... the symbol of this struggle [between the masters and the slaves]... is 'Rome against Judea, Judea against Rome'... The Romans were the strong and aristocratic; a nation stronger and more aristocratic has never existed in the world, has never been dreamed of... The Jews, conversely, were that priestly nation of resentment par excellence, possessed by a unique genius for popular morals... It is at least certain that *sub hoc signo* Israel, with its revenge and transvaluation of all values, has up to the present always triumphed again over all other ideals, over all more aristocratic ideals... all that has been done on earth against 'the noble,' 'the powerful,' 'the masters,' 'the rulers,' fades into nothing compared with what the Jews have done against them."[37]

35 Friedrich Nietzsche, *Antichrist*, p. 83.
36 Friedrich Nietzsche, *Thus Spoke Zarathustra*, p. 249.
37 Friedrich Nietzsche, *On the Genealogy of Morals*, pp. 31-33, 53-54.

Nietzsche accused the Jews—and later the Christians—of having produced, from their resentment and their vengeful sentiment, this moral revolution which constituted the most incredible and meticulous falsification of morality and history, through a total transvaluation of the noble pagan values. That is how the *pia fraus*—the "sacred lie"—was born, that is, Christian morality and its false ideals, which will be the beginning of nihilism, i.e. the negation of this life and the invention of an afterlife and a transcendent and unreachable God: "This people [the Jews] used the *pia fraus* with such perfection, such 'good conscience' that we couldn't be wary enough when it preaches morality."[38]

Nietzsche considered that the Jews have distorted nature and reality, they have transformed themselves into a living antithesis of natural conditions, they have literally turned history, religion and morality upside down; indeed, the Jew "devalues, desacralises nature: it is at this sole price that he exists... all the values of the Church are recognised for what they are, the most perverse falsification possible, with the sole aim of devaluing nature and natural values."[39]

This anti-natural religion which gradually ruled the ancient world, replacing the ancient natural pagan religion, has led to decadence, to the sickness of mankind; the final aim was to "make mankind sick, and to invert—in order to better threaten life and denigrate the world—the notions of 'good' and 'evil,' of 'true' and 'false.' The history of Israel is irreplaceable as a history of the denaturalisation of all natural values."[40]

Jewish hate, "that most profound and sublime hate, which creates ideals and changes old values to new creations, the like of which has never been on earth,"[41] this hatred of the weak has led the Jews to accomplish the miracle of a total inversion of values:

> The Jews achieved that miracle of inversion of values thanks to which life on earth has for a couple of millennia acquired a new and dangerous fascination- their prophets fused "rich," "godless," "evil," "violent," "sensual" into one and were the first to coin the word "world" as a word of infamy. It is in this inversion of values (with which is involved the employment of the word for "poor" as a synonym of "holy" and

---

38 Friedrich Nietzsche, *The Will to Power*, p. 181.

39 Friedrich Nietzsche, *Antichrist*, pp. 39, 51.

40 Ibid., p. 36.

41 Friedrich Nietzsche, *On the Genealogy of Morals*, p. 32.

"friend") that the significance of the Jewish people resides: with them begins the slave revolt in morals.[42]

This total inversion of values, which reflects the will to power of the priest who wants to vanquish his old Roman masters through lies and deception, aimed to replace the morality of the natural, pagan and aristocratic religion of the Romans with that of Christianity, a religion for weak souls, characters, and spirits:

> The Jews, that priestly nation which eventually realised that the one method of effecting satisfaction on its enemies and tyrants was by means of a radical transvaluation of values, which was at the same time an act of the cleverest revenge. That was the only way which befitted this priestly nation, this nation of the most profound priestly vengeance. It was the Jews who, in opposition to the aristocratic equation (good = aristocratic = beautiful = happy = loved by the gods), dared with a terrifying logic to suggest the contrary equation, and indeed to maintain with the teeth of the most profound hatred (the hatred of weakness) this contrary equation, namely, "the wretched are alone the good; the poor, the weak, the lowly, are alone the good; the suffering, the needy, the sick, the loathsome, are the only ones who are pious, the only ones who are blessed, for them alone is salvation—but you, on the other hand, you aristocrats, you men of power, you are to all eternity the evil, the horrible, the covetous, the insatiate, the godless; eternally also shall you be unblessed, the cursed, the damned!"[43]

That is how, according to Nietzsche, "it was, in fact, with the Jews that the revolt of the slaves begins in the sphere of morals; that revolt which has behind it a history of two millennia, and which at the present day has only moved out of our sight, because it has achieved victory."[44]

Thus began the negation of *this* world through the invention of *another world* as the sole hope for all the oppressed of the earth. Christianity has led to a systematic negation of nature and of life, and hence to nihilism, that is, a real moral and existential suicide. The "other" world thus became the "real world," and the world in which we live became an illusion. After having inverted all natural values, Christianity finally set

42 Friedrich Nietzsche, *Par-delà Bien et Mal* (*Beyond Good and Evil*), (Paris: Gallimard, 1971), p. 119.

43 Friedrich Nietzsche, *On the Genealogy of Morals*, p. 31.

44 Ibid., p. 32.

out to deny the real world as a culmination of this moral and spiritual falsification: God thus became unreachable to man, in contrast to the immanent God of polytheist pantheism which characterised the ancient pagan religions.

In order to better understand how the natural pagan and ancient values have been inverted, culminating in the invention of a God "in heaven," it is important to closely examine and analyse paragraph 14 of Nietzsche's first book *On the Genealogy of Morals*, in which he gauges "the abyss and the very depths" of religious ideals, that is, the process of fabrication of the ideals of slave morality, which has been the predominant morality since the advent of Christianity. It is a sort of descent into hell which Nietzsche invites us to undertake in order to gauge the origin of morality:

> Does anyone wish to gaze for a moment into the secret where earthly ideals are fabricated? Who has the courage to do so? … Let's go! Here we have a view of this obscure apothecary.[45]

One notices the words "obscure apothecary" which Nietzsche chooses to illustrate the process of fabrication of morality, a process which he compares to the place where the apothecary sells, stocks and prepares his herbs and medicines; hence morality, in the final analysis, is just a medicine, a remedy for the sick, the weak and the suffering, who view and live life as a curse. Life itself is a sickness which can only be cured by the moral remedy, the ascetic ideal, which in the final analysis is merely an illusion and a lie (a "deceiving sparkle," as Nietzsche says) invented to escape life.

Thus, morality, to Nietzsche, is itself a sickness, a poison prepared by the sick—the moralists—for the sick, that is, the weaklings and those who suffer. Only the bold man, who has the courage to face reality, ventures into this "abyss of ideals" to try to discover the origin of morality. We notice Nietzsche's sarcasm and contempt as he searches for ideals not in the higher spheres where they are supposed to dwell, but in the "abyss," in the dark depths of an abject humanity. Indeed, in the following passage, Nietzsche writes: "I do not see anything, hence I hear better… they want to present weakness as a merit."[46]

---

45 Friedrich Nietzsche, *On the Genealogy of Morals*, p. 47.
46 Ibid.

Darkness represents deceit and baseness of spirit and intention. That is how weakness turns into "merit" in this obscure apothecary; being weak becomes a compliment, a virtue, an ideal to pursue and to emulate. It is a veritable inversion of ancient aristocratic values that Christian morality undertakes: one wants to "pass weakness off as 'goodness'; the most fearful baseness as 'humility'; submission to those who are hated, as 'obedience'... what is inoffensive in the weak, his abundant cowardice... is here advantageously called 'patience,' sometimes even virtue; not-to-be-able-to-take-revenge is called not-to-want-to-take-revenge, maybe even forgive."[47]

Thus, weakness is transformed into "goodness," fearful baseness into "humility," submission into obedience towards "God." Nietzsche condemns this gregarious instinct of obedience, this spirit of submission before the moral imperative "thou shalt," which is what led—according to him—to the herd European man, to modernity's docile and submissive "human cattle"[48] or bovine mankind; cowardice becomes patience, virtue.

In addition, one notices that Nietzsche always puts between quotes the Christian ideals ("goodness," "humility," "obedience," "patience," etc.) which he considers to be lies deceitfully disguised in the form of eternal truths and virtues. One clearly notices the hypocrisy of the "good" who is good not out of choice, but out of weakness, who is good because he doesn't have the power to be evil; and who has the nerve to transform his incapacity to take revenge into a free and noble will *not* to take revenge.

Consequently, according to Christianity, only the suffering and the weak are "good," and they need morals to justify their weakness, and, what is more, to transform it into the very essence of goodness, selflessness and nobility. The *Agnus Dei* becomes the example to follow, the model for mankind.

As for the Christian exhortation to "love thine enemy," Nietzsche condemns it and accuses it of being motivated by fear and utilitarianism (and hence of being artificial, fake), and not by nobility or selfless compassion, as was the case for Jesus, the "only and last Christian." This so-called Christian "love" is thus not a superior goodness inherent in Christian man, but rather a mask behind which the weak of character,

---

47 Ibid., p. 48.
48 Friedrich Nietzsche, *Beyond Good and Evil*, pp. 122-123.

the powerless and the spineless protects himself against those who are stronger than him.

The process of fabrication of Christian "ideals" — and of falsification of natural values — continues thus:

> They are miserable... all these counterfeiters, although they keep each other warm, — yet they tell me that their misery is an election and a sign of distinction which they have received from God, who loves well chastises well; maybe this misery is also a preparation, a challenge, a learning — maybe even more, something which one day will be compensated and reimbursed with enormous interest in gold, no! in happiness... that is what they call "beatitude."[49]

These men "warmly curled up against each other," these weak hypocrites, fabricators of lies, are for Nietzsche the miserable, the scum of the earth, the real "poor spirits"; and it is their arrogance which strikes him the most: these wretched creatures transform their poverty of spirit, their misery, into an election and a divine distinction, into "beatitude" which becomes an ideal, a promise of *petit bourgeois* bliss which all the other miserable people can buy — in the form of exorbitant donations to the Church.

Misery thus becomes a privilege ("one whips the dog that one loves best"), for it allows those who suffer the most in this world to find beatitude in the hereafter (at a price that the church decides; bliss can hence be bought, according to the priests, these shop-keepers of the spirit). In *Antichrist*, Nietzsche refutes the "humanitarian benefits" of the Church, accusing it on the contrary of exploiting the misery of the others in order to perpetuate itself: "It was too contrary to its deepest interest to abolish whatever misery there is, it lived off misery, it created misery in order to perpetuate itself."[50]

The progression of the process of invention of values undertaken by the priests reaches grotesque dimensions; thus, "not only are they better... than the masters of the earth, the powerful whose boots they should lick (not out of fear, not at all out of fear! But because God commands that one should submit to his authority), not only are they better,

49 Friedrich Nietzsche, *On the Genealogy of Morals*, p. 48.
50 Friedrich Nietzsche, *Antichrist*, p. 87.

they are 'better gifted'... what a poisoned atmosphere! This apothecary where one produces ideals — it seems to me that it reeks of lies."[51]

Ironically, the priests — who perfectly embody the spirit of the slave — pretend to be better than, and even superior to, the powerful and the masters (that is, to the free spirits, the strong souls, the tragic men who do not need morality and accept life as it is), even though they are obliged to "lick their boots" (this expression clearly shows Nietzsche's contempt for the servility of the priests towards the kings and the aristocrats). One notices the contrast between what they pretend and what they do, hence their petty hypocrisy. Nietzsche scoffs at this hypocrisy of priests who pretend to obey not out of fear but out of respect for the scriptures, for God's word which commands them to obey ("give to Caesar what is Caesar's"). Thus, the priests hide their cowardice and their powerlessness, justifying their servility with these words while pretending to be superior to those whom they humbly serve. But they do not stop there, they go further, and that is what offends Nietzsche the most, for these people now pretend that they are "better gifted," that they are the elect; or that, "in any case, they shall be better gifted one day," that is, in "paradise" — did not Jesus say "the last will be the first"? Outraged, Nietzsche declares all this to be mere lies and illusions.

Further on in the aforementioned passage, Nietzsche describes the resentment which gnaws at the priests and which pushes them to invert all reality in order to take revenge on their masters:

> No! One more moment! You still haven't said anything about the masterpiece of these magicians who fabricate whiteness, milk and innocence with any black... these subterranean animals which are but vengeance and hatred, what do they indeed do with vengeance and hatred? Have you heard such words? If you were to trust only their words, would you have doubted that you were simply amid men of resentment![52]

The priest is thus a perverted alchemist of morality, a sorcerer, an expert in lies who inverts values, a subterranean beast full of vengeance and hatred, who perfectly embodies Christian resentment which turns all values into non-values and, vice versa, who uses morality as an instrument of vengeance against the strong and the mighty of character and of spirit (and not only of mere privileged social status); and what better

---

51 Friedrich Nietzsche, *On the Genealogy of Morals*, p. 48.
52 Ibid., p. 49.

revenge of the weak than that which inverts values, turning the slave into the master?

Thus, Nietzsche considers that Christianity is a religion born from the resentment of the weak and the oppressed against the strong, a religion which has undertaken an inversion of all values. The priests disguise their vengeance and their hatred in love and in forgiveness in order to better enslave mankind and domesticate the strong, by making them Christians, that is, weak and submitting to the authority of the Church.

Moreover, these liberated slaves now proclaim themselves the "just of the earth":

> I understand, I once again open my ears (and I hold my nose!). Now, finally, I understand what they have said so many times: "We the good—we are the just"—what they demand, they do not call it reprisals, but "triumph of justice"; what they hate is not their enemy, no! They hate "injustice," "impiety"; their hope, their faith, is not the hope of vengeance, the intoxication of sweet vengeance ("sweeter than honey," as Homer already called it), but the victory of God, of the just God over the impious; what is still left for them to love in the world are not their brothers in hatred, but their "brothers in love," as they say, all the good and the just in the world.[53]

Nietzsche "holds his nose" because of foul smells emanating from these sick lower depths of mankind. After having inverted all values, the priests end up proclaiming their ultimate victory over life, over a healthy and strong humanity. Still hiding their resentment behind the ideals of goodness and humility, they call their vengeance against the strong "the triumph of justice," and show their hatred for their enemies, the strong, by condemning "injustice" and "impiety" (thus we go back to the hypocritical Christian love of one's enemies which, according to Nietzsche, is nothing but disguised hatred stemming from cowardice and powerlessness). All that which serves their ambition to wreak vengeance takes the form of ideals to pursue, and all that which constitutes an obstacle to it becomes immorality and sin.

Therefore, the victory of God, of the just over the impious, hides the hope, the intoxication of sweet revenge, a revenge of epic proportions, given that it reminds us of Homer. The priests pretend to love not their brothers in hatred, those who are like them, but their brothers in love.

---

53 Ibid.

What the priests call "the good and the just of the world" are in fact, for Nietzsche, like them, men of resentment, weak men who feel only hatred towards the strong and desire nothing but revenge, hypocritically disguised as morality. Nietzsche continues.

> And what do they call that which serves as a consolation in all of life's sufferings — the illusion of their anticipation of future beatitude? What now? Have I heard right? They call it "last judgment," the advent of their kingdom, of the "kingdom of God" — meanwhile, however, they "live in faith," "in love," "in hope." — Enough! Enough![54]

The "last judgment," the "kingdom of God" is the culminating point of the process of inversion of values undertaken by the priests; it is their consolation and their fantasy, their hallucinatory promise of a better life in the hereafter, in an undefined future, in order to allay their suffering and make life on earth more bearable. It is *their* reign, their futuristic utopia. But in the meantime, the only way they can bear existence and domesticate and rule the strong, is to live "in faith, in love, in hope," as their book, the Evangel, prescribes.

The process of inversion of values, the Christian lie, thus culminates in the afterlife, what Nietzsche calls "the will to negate all reality," the "void," the negation of life. That is why Christianity is to him the worst of corruptions, for, by inventing a beyond and by giving value only to this "kingdom of heaven," while despising the *only* and *real* life, has led to nihilism, to the negation of this world and of oneself. That is why Nietzsche exclaims "enough, enough" of this millenarian lie which has put mankind in a moral coma from which it is only starting to awaken after having realised, accepted and transcended the death of God, as Nietzsche did.

-III- The death of God, or the end of the millenarian lie: End or perpetuation of nihilism?

The nihilism caused by the life-denying Christian morality logically and naturally led to the death of this false "God," a death which became necessary, given that it represented the end of the "longest error": the notion of a transcendent and moral God. Thus ended the "millenarian

---

54 Ibid., pp. 49-50.

lie," man having finally realised that what he had been venerating for two thousand years was in fact only an illusion.

Indeed, Nietzsche considered that when man will realise that he was "stripped of his divinity instead of being elevated to it, a deep open chasm which only a miracle can cross, the prostration which is caused by the deepest self-loathing,"[55] it is then that nihilism will descend upon humanity and the death of God will ensue as a logical consequence of this nihilism.

Man (at least the enlightened man), finally awaking from his millenarian dream of a "kingdom of heaven" in a "beyond," will then realise that what he was venerating for millennia were mere chimera and illusions, and will ask himself, as Nietzsche did, "and what if it turns out that God himself had been our longest lie?"[56] to finally conclude with him that "God today is a mere fading word, not even a concept,"[57] and to finally proclaim "the end of the longest error," of the "real world."[58]

The death of the Christian god and of Christian morality, both life-denying and anti-natural, had thus become a necessity for mankind, which had to choose between being and not being: "eliminate your venerations, or… eliminate yourselves,"[59] Nietzsche exhorts us in *The Gay Science*. He also writes in *The Will to Power*: "Morality is the life-negating instinct. We must destroy morality to liberate life."[60]

Further on, Nietzsche declares: "mankind, for millennia, has venerated mere lies as truths," thus "a good dose of immoralism was necessary in order to give the signal of aggression, I mean reason."[61] This immoralism is the death of God, killed by reason. Man has therefore chosen to destroy his veneration instead of destroying himself. To Nietzsche, the death of the Judeo-Christian god represents the rejection of nihilism, the refusal to destroy ourselves, the will to *live*, to live *this* life, *real* life, in its totality, with its pains and joys, its glory and its misery.

The death of the moral god of monotheism therefore represents the culmination but perhaps also the refusal and the end of nihilism, given that it henceforth allows man to sail towards new horizons and thus

---

55   Friedrich Nietzsche, *The Will to Power*, vol. I, p. 187.
56   Friedrich Nietzsche, *The Gay Science*, p. 283.
57   Friedrich Nietzsche, *The Will to Power*, vol. I, p. 194.
58   Friedrich Nietzsche, *Twilight of the idols*, pp. 82-83.
59   Friedrich Nietzsche, *The Gay Science*, p. 288.
60   Friedrich Nietzsche, *The Will to Power*, vol. I, p. 137.
61   Ibid., p. 153.

opens the way to a new era, which could either be better (if nihilism is transcended and vanquished), or worse (if man sinks into a second nihilism caused by the absence of a goal) than the Christian era, depending on the attitude man adopts facing this death.

Indeed, the deicide, the assassination of God, even of a false god, is an act of epic proportions, with heavy consequences for mankind. The divine death leaves behind it a huge existential chasm and reveals to man his cosmic solitude; distraught, confused, lost, man asks himself: "And now? What is the meaning of life? What new meaning must life have?"

In the absence of an answer, the inferior—or even ordinary—man sinks into despair, into a second nihilism provoked this time by the crisis of meaning that positivist rationalism suffers from, being totally devoid of all higher end, of all spirituality, and characterised by an absolute scepticism, or what Nietzsche calls "the pessimism of the weak." In this case, nihilism—which had pushed man to "kill" God (human reason having revolted against Christianity's infantile lies and superstitions)—nihilism perpetuates itself following the divine death, the fact which plunges humanity in an unbearable void. The following quotation from *The Gay Science* perfectly illustrates the immeasurable catastrophe which has befallen mankind:

> Where has God gone? ... I shall tell you. We have killed him—you and I. We are all his murderers! But how have we done this? How were we able to drink up the sea? Who gave us the sponge to wipe away the entire horizon? What did we do when we unchained the earth from its sun? Whither is it moving now? Whither are we moving now? Away from all suns? Are we not perpetually falling? Backward, sideward, forward, in all directions? Is there any up or down left? Are we not straying as through an infinite nothing? Do we not feel the breath of empty space? Has it not become colder? Is it not more and more night coming on all the time? Must not lanterns be lit in the morning? Do we not hear anything yet of the noise of the gravediggers who are burying God? Do we not smell anything yet of God's decomposition? Gods too decompose! God is dead! God remains dead! And we have killed him![62]

The death of God is thus a veritable "solar eclipse" for which the whole of mankind is responsible (Nietzsche only *discerns* this death, he is *not* God's "murderer"); and the *horror vacui* (the "horror of the void")

---

62 Friedrich Nietzsche, *The Gay Science*, p. 166.

inherent in man pushes him to ask himself how to face this second nihilism, much worse than the first (for it is without any hope), how to face this absolute void of life following the death of God? How to live in a world devoid of meaning?

Must one accept to sink in nothingness, or even to *seek* nothingness (the Nirvana) as the only way to escape earthly sufferings, as Schopenhauer and the Buddhists, these staunch pessimists, had done? That, Nietzsche believes, would be to deny life once more; indeed, according to him, Buddhism is just another form of Christianity—albeit superior to and less decadent than Christianity—and thus another form of nihilism, a pessimistic doctrine (and of the pessimism of the weak, not of the strong) which denies this life and leads man to a veritable spiritual suicide as the only way to escape a life devoid of meaning and full of suffering.

The "slave," that is, the superstitious, weak, suffering man, needs an egalitarian transcendent god before whom all could—and should—be equal; he also needs "the other world" to compensate for the injustice of which he thinks he is the victim in this life. Thus, after having realised the death of this "God" which he feared and venerated, this god which represented his sole hope of a better life and reparation of justice, the weak finds refuge in Buddhism and preaches the annihilation of the ego and the negation of this world which he views as *maya*, as an illusion, as the sole escape from this hell that is the life of the weak and the inferior.

To Nietzsche, that is not the solution, for he considers that Buddhism, although softer, deeper and less hypocritical than Christianity, nonetheless only perpetuates nihilism and does not transcend it.

Positive realism, or the reign of the last man

What to do then? How do we overcome the death of God? Must we live a hedonistic, depraved, amoral life, the only escape for these secular slaves, these modern Epicureans that are the positivist materialists, the so-called "realists" who believe in nothing because—as Nietzsche says—they are "unworthy of belief"? Those who pretend to welcome the death of God as a liberation, but who in the final analysis have only replaced Christian morality with its secular and hedonistic version, liberal democracy, which itself has only replaced God with morality?

Must we become modern men, Nietzsche's "last men," that is, utilitarians who, for Nietzsche, are only "involuntary slaves," "fragments of men,"[63] whose narrow rationalism and search for bovine comfort and happiness offer mankind no alternative to God, no higher goal? No, for that would be to submit to a new dogma, another form of orthodoxy, the idolatry of cold reason which, on its own, has never accomplished anything great; and, consequently, that would be to sink — as the Buddhists and other pessimists have done — in a second nihilism.

Indeed, it must be noted that if Nietzsche rejected the infantile dogmatism of medieval theocracy, he also equally despised Cartesian positivism which he considered had not been able to overcome nihilism, as it could not provide mankind with a viable alternative. According to Nietzsche, this led to the crisis of meaning and purpose characterising modernity, a crisis which followed the crisis of reason and freedom during the theocratic tyranny of the Middle Ages.

In *The Birth of Tragedy*, Nietzsche speaks of the "eternal struggle between the theocratic and the tragic vision of the world," arguing that it is "only after the scientific spirit, which reached its own limits, had to recognise, by noticing these limits, the nothingness of its pretention to a universal aptitude," that it would be "permitted to hope in a rebirth of tragedy,"[64] meaning a spiritual renaissance in a West paralysed by the dogma of the absolute supremacy of reason which renders all spirituality impossible.

To Nietzsche, the age of the "Enlightenment" had only replaced theocratic tyranny and morality with the orthodoxy of reason and the mediocrity and levelling character of liberalism: the Christian God was Spirit, the modern God is Reason (Hegel: "God is reason in history").

Nietzsche's philosophy is thus a repudiation of the entire humanist paradigm (both liberal and socialist) which has been predominant in the West since the Enlightenment and especially since the French Revolution. Indeed, even though his proclamation of the "death of God" was the clear and logical reaction of an enlightened philosopher rejecting the infantile notion of the transcendental Christian god, Nietzsche nonetheless believed that the Enlightenment's positivist and Cartesian rationalism, with its narrow and limited "realism" and utilitarianism, was surely not the alternative for civilisation, for its denial of all human

---

63 "I consider all utilitarians as involuntary slaves. Fragments of men: that is what signals the slaves." Friedrich Nietzsche, *The Will to Power*, p. 262.

64 Friedrich Nietzsche, *La Naissance de la Tragédie* (*The Birth of Tragedy*) (Paris: Librairie Générale Française, 1994), p. 131.

perfection and grandeur irreversibly leads to mediocrity and even to nihilism.

Consequently, Nietzsche thought that positivist rationalism could never contribute to the elevation of man, let alone to the creation of the Superman as mankind's supreme goal, producing instead only "men without chests," that is, modernity's contemptible race of sterile and mediocre "realists" with petty virtues and flat and empty souls:

> For thus you speak: "we are complete realists, and without belief or superstition": thus you thump your chests — alas, even without having chests! But how could you be able to believe, you motley-spotted men! — You who are paintings of all that has ever been believed! You are walking refutations of belief itself and the fracture of all thought. Unworthy of belief: that is what I call you, you realists! All ages babble in confusion in your spirits; and the dreaming and babbling of all ages was more real than is your waking! You are unfruitful: therefore you lack belief. But he who had to create always had his prophetic dreams and star-auguries — and he believed in belief![65]

Nietzsche's philosophy is thus a pagan, neo-classical and neo-aristocratic revolt against the humanist tradition of the West, that is, against Judeo-Christianity, rationalism, socialism, and liberalism. However, it should also be noted in this context that Nietzsche despised just as much chauvinist, narrow, "bovine" nationalism, describing the state as the "coldest of all cold monsters" created for the "superfluous" masses, and proudly proclaiming himself a "good European" and advocating the establishment of a world government dominated by a universal caste of masters (as we shall see in the next chapter).

Therefore, Nietzsche's flagrant and deep contempt for liberal democracy led him to break all links with Judeo-Christian Western civilisation, whose purely materialistic, selfish, petty, utilitarian "virtues" reject Man's real mission on this earth, which is none other than self-perfection and self-overcoming.

In order to transcend and overcome nihilism, one must thus avoid sinking in a second nihilism represented by a world which, under the tyranny of "cold reason," remains devoid of meaning, a world which lacks a higher end that goes beyond the immediate material needs and petty pleasures of a soulless civilisation devoid of belief. This world

---

65 Friedrich Nietzsche, *Thus Spoke Zarathustra*, p. 154.

which Nietzsche condemns is the product of the rationalism of the "Enlightenment" and of the ideals of the French revolution, "that gruesome and superfluous farce" with superficial and materialist values which was in fact merely the "daughter and the continuation of Christianity... it has that same instinct which is hostile to castes, to aristocrats, to the last privileges,"[66] given that, through its slogan "liberty, equality, fraternity," it only perpetuated the Christian lie of the "equality of souls before God" and thus corrupted mankind by declaring a total war on all that is noble and lofty.

Rejecting both socialism and liberalism as two aspects of the same materialist and egalitarian vision of the world—a vision which is at the same time individualistic and egalitarian[67]—Nietzsche condemns the levelling character of these theories which, according to him, have led to a general levelling and "mediocrisation" as well as a real cult of the ugly and the base by establishing the "lie of the equality of souls before God" as the main foundation of society. Socialism, "the tyranny of the least and the dumbest, of the superficial and envious,"[68] naively dreams of establishing a classless society by imposing the "injustice" of "equal rights for everyone," thus violating the aristocratic principle of nature; consequently, the spirit of the herd embodied by the humanist values leads to the decline of mankind instead of achieving so-called "progress":

These honourable values which are called "humanity," "mankind," "compassion," "pity," surely have a superficial value in that they weaken and soften certain dangerous and powerful instincts; but in the long run they only lead to the debasement of man—mediocrify him, if I am allowed that desperate word in a desperate situation... the human comedy would consist in that Europeans, thanks to their growing morality, believe in all innocence and in all vanity that they are elevating themselves whereas in truth they are declining; I mean to say that, by developing all the virtues that benefit the herd and by rejecting the opposite virtues, which alone mould a superior race, stronger and more dominating, they only develop in man the herd beast and maybe contribute to

---

66 Friedrich Nietzsche, *The Will to Power*, vol. I, p. 160.

67 "The individual is an infinitely vulnerable vanity; knowing how much it is prone to suffer, this vanity leads him to demand that all men be recognised as equal, that he find himself *inter pares*. The individualistic principle eliminates the very great men." Friedrich Nietzsche, *The Will to Power*, vol. II, p. 95.

68 Friedrich Nietzsche, *The Will to Power*, vol. I, p. 211.

"define" the human animal—for until now man has been "the animal which is not yet defined."[69]

Against socialism, Nietzsche directs the worst of accusations, that of wanting to deny life through "the general degeneration of mankind, its debasement to the level of what the louts and flat heads of socialism hold for 'future man'—their ideal!—this decadence and this belittling of man transformed into a herd beast (man, as they say, is of the 'free society'), this animalisation of men reduced to the rank of dwarfs all having the same rights and the same needs."[70]

As for the liberals, Nietzsche does not spare them either—just as he would spare no one, he the ruthless "hammer" which breaks idols, prophet of a new philosophy of life destined for a higher species that is yet to be born. Nietzsche described the liberals as the "feebler descendants" of communists and socialists. Liberal democracy, which is "Christianity made natural"—albeit in a secular and modern version—also stands guilty of instituting the "superstition" of the "equality of all before God."

To Nietzsche, liberalism—just like socialism—represents mediocrity and the animalisation of man, who thus becomes an "involuntary slave" (as we have already seen), given the egalitarian and levelling character of this theory, in addition to its narrow, selfish and petty individualism, which reduces man to a simple—albeit presumptuous—atom in a mediocre and shallow society which lacks a vision of the world and a higher goal; consequently, liberalism has never produced great men—nor will it ever—given that it strives to eliminate them.

By declaring that "human society is an experiment... not a 'contract'!", exhorting his "brothers" to "break" such a word, a word for "soggy hearts and men of half-measure,"[71] Nietzsche launches a scathing attack against liberalism's "contract theory" inspired by Locke, Hobbes and Rousseau, forerunners to the French Revolution and its concept of the herd-state which, for socialists and democrats, is but an instrument for the levelling of men, and for creating a sort of pseudo-aristocracy of money, an oligarchy consisting of mediocre, selfish, and materialistic men.

---

69 Friedrich Nietzsche, *The Will to Power*, vol. II, pp. 94-95.
70 Friedrich Nietzsche, *Beyond Good and Evil*, p. 131.
71 Friedrich Nietzsche, *Thus Spoke Zarathustra*, p. 263.

Thus, liberalism represents the rule of money and the "herd-animalisation,"[72] while democracy represents majority rule. Consequently, both lead to the levelling and "mediocrisation" of man, turning him into a servile and unconscious "herd-animal." This animalisation, according to Nietzsche, is accomplished through the institutions of parliamentary democracy, which is decadence assuming a political form, and which incarnates, in Nietzsche's own words, "the unbelief in great men and in the elite. 'Each is equal to each.' Basically, we're all the same herd, the same selfish mob," whereas aristocracy represents "the belief in a human elite and a superior caste."[73] Nietzsche does not care for the value—let alone the dignity—of ordinary man, the goal being "not mankind but the Superman."

Thus, Nietzsche makes a clear distinction between the healthy, higher, "heroic" egoism of great men and exceptional individuals, and the lower petty selfishness of the liberals. "Egoism," for the higher man, is the drive to increase the power of the soul, to rise higher and to perpetually overcome himself and create beyond himself. Man's highest elevation is the attainment of his individuality, yet this process is limited to the select few born with noble souls, for whom happiness is self-overcoming, and not the mere bovine comfort and sterile self-preservation so characteristic of common "herdmen."

Nietzsche's politics is in this sense neither collectivistic nor individualistic in the narrow sense, for he considers that liberal individualism does not recognise the order of rank and levels men by imposing equal rights on all; in much the same way, collectivism, or communitarianism, does not believe in great men, because of its egalitarian and levelling character which breeds and generalises mediocrity.

To make sure his "heroic individualism" would not be confused with democratic or liberal individualism (selfishness would be a more accurate term), Nietzsche, without naming it (but strongly implying it), contrasts the Germanic noble, higher freedom or "*Freiheit*" with the Anglo-Saxon liberal atomistic conception of "liberty," which is shallow, selfish, utilitarian and hedonistic. *Freiheit* is a much deeper, more philosophical concept which bears a spiritual dimension and implies self-overcoming. It is the freedom of the master, the higher man who looks at humanity from above, from his heights.

---

72 Friedrich Nietzsche, *Twilight of the Idols*, p. 83.
73 Friedrich Nietzsche, *The Will to Power*, p. 243.

Thus, Nietzsche condemns and despises the liberal atomistic concept of freedom, which is largely prevalent nowadays (especially in the Anglo-Saxon world); instead of this empty and superficial notion of freedom, Nietzsche affirms his own idea of freedom as victory, higher freedom, the freedom of the warrior of the spirit ("the free man is a warrior," Nietzsche declares in *Twilight of the Idols*),[74] a freedom which lies in self-overcoming, struggle, the will to power in the service of a higher thought and a supreme goal:

> Do you call yourself free? I want to hear your ruling idea, and not that you have escaped from a yoke... Free from what? Zarathustra does not care about that! But your eye should clearly tell me: free for what?[75]

A "free spirit," to Nietzsche, as we shall see in the next chapter, represents a very different species than that of the liberals, "of another kind than those who hitherto have called themselves free spirits, for those wanted nearly the opposite."[76] Nietzsche's conception of freedom is therefore radically different from that of the democrats and liberals; Nietzsche in fact believes that liberal institutions hamper freedom:

> Nothing is more systematically nefarious to freedom than liberal institutions. One knows well what they lead to: they weaken the will to power, they turn the levelling of the heights and the base depths into a moral system, they render petty, cowardly and pleasurable—in them, the herd animal always triumphs.[77]

Thus, Nietzsche despises the notion of freedom as advocated by democrats, for it is merely a freedom from constraint, freedom "from a yoke," and not a freedom which strives after perfection and self-overcoming. He condemns the so-called liberal positivist "free thinkers" who mistakenly and deceitfully claim to be "free spirits" (calling them instead "fake free spirits") as a type that is "unfree" and very superficial, considering them to be "levellers" who staunchly fight for "equality of rights for all" and for "sympathy for all those who suffer," in order to achieve the "universal

---

74 Friedrich Nietzsche, *Twilight of the Idols*, p. 83.
75 Friedrich Nietzsche, *Thus Spoke Zarathustra*, pp. 84-85.
76 Friedrich Nietzsche, *The Will to Power*, vol. II, p. 273.
77 Friedrich Nietzsche, *Twilight of the Idols*, p. 83.

green pasture happiness of the herd, with security, safety, comfort and an easier life for all."[78]

Socialism, liberalism, democracy: for Nietzsche, these doctrines, which are secularised, modern versions of Judeo Christianity, are responsible for leading humanity towards the era of decadence and mediocrity: modernity, which represents the "victory of the slaves" and of their "petty virtues," mob rule: "does this present not belong to the mob?" deplores Nietzsche, adding: "Mob above, mob below! What are 'poor' and 'rich' today! I unlearned that distinction."[79]

Indeed, despite shallow differences of form, not of nature and essence, socialism and liberalism belong—in Nietzsche's eyes—to the same materialist and egalitarian "decadent" paradigm, producing a level-ling—and hence, a degeneration and animalisation—of society which symbolises "the instinct of the herd, that is, a sum of zeroes—where every zero has 'equal rights,' where it is virtuous to be zero."[80]

"Equal rights for all" is thus the "greatest injustice, for the greatest men find themselves frustrated."[81] Consequently, Nietzsche declares an all-out war on positivist realism (i.e. Cartesian rationalism), a doctrine which prevents man from elevating and overcoming himself and thus transcending God's death, in order to enable one day the creation of the Superman, the ultimate goal of mankind, according to Nietzsche. Socialism and liberalism thus represent the rule of "men without chests," the victory of the "Last Man," who is the "beginning of the end," that is, the despicable herd-man of modernity:

> Alas! The time is coming when man will give birth to no more stars. Alas! The time of the most contemptible man is coming... Behold! I shall show you the Ultimate Man. The earth has become small, and upon it hops the Ultimate Man, who makes everything small.[82]

Indeed, according to Nietzsche, we are living in the "era of the slave," the age of the "Last Man" (the latter being the antithesis to the Superman), a mediocre age devoid of meaning and greatness. By imposing a secular version of the Christian slogan of the "equality of souls before God," the

---

78 Friedrich Nietzsche, *The Will to Power*, vol. II, p. 272.

79 Friedrich Nietzsche, *Thus Spoke Zarathustra*, p. 327.

80 Friedrich Nietzsche, *The Will to Power*, vol. I, p. 211.

81 Ibid., vol. II, p. 250.

82 Friedrich Nietzsche, *Thus Spoke Zarathustra*, p. 26.

French Revolution, "that gruesome farce," gave birth to socialism and liberalism, two egalitarian twin sisters which have reduced man into a spiritual dwarf, a modern slave.

The Judeo-Christian transcendent, unreachable, life-denying god prevented all human perfection on earth, in the here and now; thus it is only after the death of the Christian god that men would be able to overcome themselves and become gods themselves, for, "precisely this is Godliness, that there are gods but no God!"[83] Indeed, man must choose between the glory of God and his own glory, and man's glory is embodied by the Superman.

However, according to Nietzsche, the materialist liberal and socialist doctrines, products of the Enlightenment, were certainly not the alternative to the transcendentalism of Christianity, their nihilist and materialist atheism rejecting all possibility of self-overcoming and self-perfection, and thus transforming man into a petty, shallow, hedonistic creature in search of the "happiness" of the herd, a slave to his desires and his instincts, instead of being their master. Positivist rationalism's absolute atheism has thus led to the "dwarfing" and "animalisation" of man, to the "Last Man," the "lord and master" of the present: "Overcome for me these masters of the present, O my brothers — these petty people: they are the Superman's greatest danger!"[84]

Thus, the age of the Superman will be a radically aristocratic, anti-democratic age. What is left to know is what kind of aristocracy Nietzsche was writing about, and how the new lords of the earth will be different from their predecessors.

The death of God as a prelude to the Superman: The higher man's attitude

As we have seen, for Nietzsche, neither Christian superstition, nor positivist materialism, nor Buddhist pessimism constitute a viable alternative to nihilism, for they only perpetuate it, they only produce semblances of men, caricatures of men. What, then, is the alternative to God? How to overcome God's death? Nietzsche believes that if man does not invent a new meaning, if he does not set a new goal for life, the death of God would have been in vain, and nihilism would be perpetuated.

---

83 Ibid., p. 252.
84 Friedrich Nietzsche, *Thus Spoke Zarathustra*, p. 348.

The death of God is at the same time a misfortune and a boon for mankind, or rather it is a misfortune for one kind of humanity and a boon for another kind. It is a misfortune for the slave, for the masses, for those who are afraid to face the truth, which is none other than this: man is alone in the world, and he alone can and must replace God; it is up to him alone to reinvent himself, to overcome himself, and to create his own god. The born slaves see in this truth a veritable call to moral, spiritual, and even physical suicide. Hence the nihilism which is prevalent nowadays after what Nietzsche calls the "victory of slave morality."

However, those who are born superior (whatever their socio-economic status may be), the "masters," the "lords" with higher souls, the noble of spirit, see with a very different eye the death of God: by "killing" God (or rather by recognising his death), all becomes possible. For the higher man, God's "death" is a real liberation from the yoke of anti-natural and dogmatic morality as well as monotheism's other millenarian lies, a new dawn which enables men to live life to the fullest, to invent a new meaning, to create their own god, and even to become gods, or rather God-Men, Supermen.

Therefore, the death of God can and should be overcome through an immanentist, pantheistic, life-affirming philosophy "beyond good and evil," something which the humanist (liberal and socialist) paradigm was unable to do, sinking instead into a second nihilism and an "animalisation" of man.

To Nietzsche, only the enlightened philosophers, the *real* free spirits, accept the divine death and welcome it as a real liberation paving the way to new horizons, a new dawn for mankind:

> Thus we philosophers and "free spirits," when we hear the news that the "old god is dead," feel illuminated as by a new dawn; our heart overflows with gratitude, amazement, premonitions, expectation. At long last the horizon appears free to us again, even if it should not be bright; at long last our ships may venture out again, venture out to face any danger; all the daring of the lover of knowledge is permitted again; the sea, our sea, lies open again; perhaps there has never yet been such an "open sea."[85]

Thus, the free spirits — in contrast to the positivist "free thinkers" — see in the death of *this* god, the Judeo-Christian god, a twilight of the idols of monotheism, idols which negate life, man, and any possibility of

---

85 Friedrich Nietzsche, *The Gay Science*, pp. 279-280.

human perfection; and, at the same time, they see in this divine death a golden opportunity for man to overcome his human, "all too human" condition, and therefore to create the Superman, the incarnation of the new mode of divinity. Hence Nietzsche exhorts post-Christian mankind to "no longer pray" but rather to "bless"![86]

"Nothing is true, everything is permitted," Nietzsche liked to repeat in his bible, *Zarathustra*. In *The Will to Power*, Nietzsche says: "man is henceforth strong enough to be ashamed of God, he can be the devil's advocate again."[87]

In the same book, he warns us: "If we do not turn the death of God into a great renunciation and a perpetual victory over ourselves, we would have to pay for this loss."[88]

In other words, Nietzsche calls on humanity to choose the tragic attitude towards life, in opposition to the nihilistic attitude; he urges us to adopt the "pessimism of strength" (which derives from the will to power, and not from weakness, as is the case with the nihilists), the "immoralism" or transvaluation of old values (in contrast to amoralism, which is the absence of values):

> Is pessimism necessarily the sign of decline, of decadence, of the failure of tired and weakened instincts? ... it seems... that this is the case for us "modern" men and Europeans? Is there a pessimism of strength? An intellectual predilection for toughness, horror, cruelty, the problems of existence, caused by an overflowing health, an overflowing existence?[89]

That is how Nietzsche advocates an "active nihilism" which, contrary to passive nihilism—which is an end in itself—is but a means to vanquish oneself, a "creative destruction." We shall analyse in depth, in the next chapter, the Nietzschean conception of active nihilism—or "nihilism that has vanquished itself." Nihilism was no doubt a necessary stage to awaken man from his metaphysical coma, but it has to be overcome, lest we want it to destroy us. This nihilist who overcomes himself is none other than Nietzsche, who describes himself thus: he is the "prophet bird for whom it is enough to look behind to tell of what shall happen; he is

---

86 Friedrich Nietzsche, *The Will to Power*, vol. I, p. 10.

87 Ibid., vol. II, p. 303.

88 Ibid., p. 160.

89 Friedrich Nietzsche, *The Birth of Tragedy*, p. 34.

the first accomplished nihilist of Europe, but having pushed nihilism in him to its limit, he put it behind him, under him, outside him."[90]

Nihilism for Nietzsche is therefore only a transitory stage which should eventually be transcended, as he explains when he talks about "a period of transitory nihilism, before the advent of the force which would enable us to invert values and to divinise and justify the apparent world [as the Buddhists and Christians call our world] as the sole existing world of becoming."[91]

The death of God is thus greeted as being good news, as "glad tidings," as a momentous event by the higher man, but, contrary to what the positivists and nihilists hold, it is not an end in itself; that is, Nietzsche's atheism is not absolute. The divine death enables the free spirit to recapture what Nietzsche calls "the innocence of becoming," by adopting a tragic, heroic attitude towards life, an *amor fati* (love of fate):

> What alone can our teaching be?—That no one gives a human being his qualities: not God, not society, not his parents or ancestor, not he himself... One is necessary, one is a piece of fate, one belongs to the whole, one is in the whole—there exists nothing which could judge, measure, compare, condemn our being, for that would be to judge, measure, compare, condemn the whole... But nothing exists apart from the whole!—That no one is any longer made accountable... this alone is the great liberation—thus alone is the innocence of becoming restored... The concept "God" has hitherto been the greatest objection to existence... We deny God; in denying God, we deny accountability: only by doing that do we redeem the world.[92]

90 Friedrich Nietzsche, *The Will to Power*, vol. I, p. 8.

91 Ibid., vol. II, p. 12.

92 Friedrich Nietzsche, *Twilight of the Idols*, pp. 45-46.

CHAPTER TWO

Beyond the Death of God:
Nihilism Vanquished by Itself

To the free spirit, the tragic man who accepts life in its totality, refusing to take refuge in false beliefs and illusory hopes, the death of the old "God" of monotheism, the false god, represents the end of the longest error. However, this death is not—or rather *should* not be (or become)—an end in itself, and thus be vain; it should on the contrary be a prelude to a new, life-affirming and creative vision of the world, a new conception of man and of divinity.

Indeed, the cosmic void left by the divine death cannot be filled, and this death cannot have a meaning, if it does not offer mankind a new goal: the Superman, the future of man; otherwise, this death would have been in vain and would constitute a perpetuation of nihilism, not its end. That is the attitude of Nietzsche's higher man, that is how the will to power of the master expresses itself—through eternal self-overcoming—in contrast to the will to power of the slave, the weak man, which expresses itself through his desire to be free and to vanquish his masters by inverting all natural values, thus creating an imaginary world in which all the failures, all the men of resentment on the earth could take refuge and console themselves from their inferiority and their suffering.

It is worth noting that, to Nietzsche, the will to power summarises all reality, all truth, *life* itself, and the higher man embodies this will at its highest level, and views the world as a life-affirming and eternally self-overcoming will to power. Indeed, Nietzsche affirms that "what determines rank, what distinguishes rank, are only quantities of power, and nothing else," adding that "what determines your rank is only the quantity of power that you are: the rest is cowardice."[93] This power is mainly found in the level of courage facing truth, in the capacity to bear the vision of a world without "God," "Truth," or other ecclesiastic idols—a

---

93 Friedrich Nietzsche, *The Will to Power*, vol. II, p. 235.

Dionysian world of eternal becoming and eternal creation, where man alone can and should determine his fate and decide whether he is a bridge towards the Superman or towards the beast. It is this "selective thought" which determines each man's rank in the Nietzschean hierarchy.

The will to power is thus the new vision of the world, the only one which is true, that is, in conformity with the natural order, and hence it is the only life principle which can replace Christian morality; that is how the higher man views life. According to Nietzsche, this will is the new morality beyond good and evil which affirms and blesses life, enabling us to transcend and vanquish nihilism.

-I- Beyond good and evil: Life as will to power

To Nietzsche, the will to power represents the creative will and affirmation of life, the only true morality, but a master morality "beyond good and evil" which culminates in the creation of the Superman.

By declaring "where I found a living being, there I found the will to power; and even in the will of the slave I found the will to be master,"[94] Nietzsche considers that the whole universe is will to power, life consists of force and energy, and man is endowed with an infinite will to create, to live, to grow and overcome himself. In short, the will to power is *the* supreme truth, the *only* truth. As such, it transcends both the contemplative, transcendental "will to truth" characteristic of the ascetic ideal as well as the "will to live" advocated by the positivist liberals, which is nothing but the desire for self-preservation and the hedonistic search for comfort and the "bovine" happiness of "herd men," as Nietzsche would say.

According to Nietzsche's radically aristocratic and perfectionist philosophy, the *real* voice of justice speaks thus: power determines rank; life is a struggle, and the goal of life is the struggle itself, an endless spiritual struggle, the "war of the spirits" pitting the select few masters, free spirits in search of perpetual creation, elevation, and self-overcoming against the "many-too-many," the superfluous, unproductive masses. Ours is a cruel world of constant, ruthless struggle where only the strongest and the best survive and rule over the amorphous populace composed of weak and base creatures: that is the aristocratic law of selection "beyond good and evil" preached by Nietzsche, that same law which Christianity

---

94 Friedrich Nietzsche, *Thus Spoke Zarathustra*, p. 148.

tried to eliminate by imposing the "lie" of the equality of all souls before the moral God.

However, it is worth noting in this context that what Nietzsche means by "power" goes way beyond mere physical, biological or political power, or Darwin's "survival of the fittest." Nietzsche's concept of power has a deeper, wider dimension and must be construed as absolute power, that is, *spiritual,* moral, mental, physical *and consequently* political power.

Moreover, the will to power is experienced differently by the master and by the slave. To the slave, the weak, lower, vulgar man, it is a mere desire for freedom and — at best — a desire to become master. But to the master, the higher man, the will to power is not a mere *desire* for power, a struggle to *attain* power (in the purely Machiavellian sense) as a simple *means* to realise one's ambitions; it is rather a spiritual energy, a state of being that one desires for itself, the cause and end of all things. It is a need to discharge an abundance of power and an overflowing energy, it is the will to bestow power.

Seen in this context, that is, from the point of view of the higher man, one could say that the Nietzschean concept of will to power is essentially a question of overcoming and has a triple dimension: firstly, it represents the overcoming of Judeo-Christian morality and its notions of good and evil as well as its transcendent and personal God, the fact which leads the higher man to undertake a transvaluation of values in favour of the master morality, in opposition to the morality of slaves which has been dominating Western civilisation since the onset of Christianity. The will to power is the origin of master morality, a hierarchical morality "beyond good and evil," that is, selective, immanent and natural, in contrast to the Christian transcendental morality which is life-denying and hostile to nature.

Secondly, the will to power entails self-overcoming, it is a spiritual quest which starts with self-mastery, that is, mastering our passions and basic instincts, and culminates in the creation of "something beyond man," a superior species of man, the Superman. Thirdly, the will to power is the desire to overcome and surpass the others (the Greek word for it is *megalothymia*) in this eternal spiritual struggle that is life.

Therefore, in accordance with this vision of life which only the strong and free spirits could bear and adopt, Nietzsche accepts the death of God, after having perceived it; he accepts it despite its disastrous consequences (for the common, mediocre man). Indeed, to the common mortals, who cannot live without a God before whom they could all be equal and they could all aspire to a better life in the hereafter, the death of God is a veritable catastrophe and represents the end of all hope and all purpose, absolute nihilism. However, Nietzsche accepts this death that he views differently; he sees, as it were, beyond this death, considering that it represents for the free man—who doesn't need God to live, to hope and to aspire after perfection—it represents a prelude to the creation of a new goal for humanity. Consequently, for the higher man, the nihilism that the divine death represents does not perpetuate itself to become an end in itself, as is the case for the nihilists and the pessimists.

Thus, Nietzsche sees in the will to power the possibility of another faith, another vision of the world, a religion for the strong (a religion that would "restore human pride"), a tragic, heroic vision which offers a new hope, a new goal: the Superman, who incarnates the "new mode of divinity," an immanent divinity which affirms life and elevates man to the divine rank, instead of degrading him to the rank of "servant of God." That is how this creative and vital will enables the higher man to overcome nihilism *through* nihilism (that is what Nietzsche calls "nihilism vanquished by itself" or the "self-overcoming of morality"); this is done through an inversion of gregarious values in order to reestablish the ancient natural order, and thus through a master morality beyond good and evil advocating an eternal and creative becoming and overcoming, a return to the "innocence of becoming" and *amor fati* (love of fate) worthy of the heroic and tragic men of antiquity.

The death of the transcendental god, or the overcoming of morality

As we have seen in the previous chapter, the transcendental God incarnated to Nietzsche an escape from life, a denial of life; consequently, to every free spirit, the death of the god of monotheism represents the end of this millenarian superstition, the end of the "longest error." It is only through the elimination of the transcendental concept of "God" as an abstract notion alien to life and to man's elevation in *this* life, that we will be able to restore the natural order which prevailed in ancient pagan times preceding the advent of Christianity, before the invention of morality. It is only thus that Christian morality, this counter-nature, this "negation of life," will cease to be "a goal of life, a goal of evolution," for, according to Nietzsche, "the concept of God was hitherto the principal objection to existence."

In other words, the "death of God" is man's greatest liberation, for it is only by "killing" (that is, noticing the "error" of) *this* metaphysical concept hostile to life that mankind can one day aspire to human perfection.

Thus, the will to power of the higher man pushes him to firmly reject the Judeo-Christian notion of a transcendent God, in contrast to Christ's original message of the "kingdom of heaven in us"—what theosophists and mystics call the "inner Christ."

It is worth noting in this context that the "atheism" which is so characteristic of Nietzsche is in fact a moral, spiritual, and even a religious (or rather a *spiritual*) position stemming from his pagan conception of divinity as immanent in nature (this notion will be elaborated in the next chapter). His refusal to believe in *a* transcendent god in no way denies that God does exist (being however immanent and accessible to man through an inner mystical experience), and that human life in itself is worth living and perfectible, contrary to the conventional atheist attitude which is generally of materialistic and nihilistic inspiration and character. Indeed, Nietzsche was *pagan*, not *atheist* (at least not in the conventional sense), despite the fact that he proclaimed himself "godless." The difference is significant, for Nietzsche believes—in his own way—in a certain form of divinity, but this belief is monistic, holistic and internal (that is, mystical), and not transcendent and external; therefore, his atheism is not absolute, not an end in itself, the death of God not being the final goal.

Nietzsche clearly shows us in his *Zarathustra* that he believes in *a* God, *his own* god, rejecting the "old" God, that is, the monotheistic traditional concept of a "God in heaven": "Away with such a god! Better no god, better to produce destiny on one's own account, better to be God oneself!" Zarathustra proclaims, and the Pope answers him: "O Zarathustra, you are more pious than you believe, with such an unbelief! Some god in you has converted you to your godlessness."[95]

The fact is that man *can* and *must* be overcome, but this overcoming is the result of his own free will; man is absolutely free to pursue his own betterment, no one else is held accountable for his success or his failure, for his elevation or his fall, as the aforementioned passage on man being part of the "whole" so beautifully illustrates. The will to power is the *only* truth, for it is the only humanly palpable, humanly conceivable truth,

---

95 Ibid., p. 316.

that is, the only immanent reality and the only goal that man should pursue, for it guarantees creativity; thus preached Nietzsche:

> Willing liberates: that is the true doctrine of will and freedom—thus Zarathustra teaches you. No more to will and no more to evaluate and no more to create! Ah, that this great lassitude may ever stay far from me![96]

Willing is thus an act of creation; through the will to power, the higher man becomes the centre of the universe (being an integral part of the whole, of the absolute), thus transcending his finite existence: "one is necessary, one is a fragment of fate, one is part of the whole, one is in that whole… outside the whole, there is nothing."

Active nihilism, or nihilism vanquished by itself

"O my brethren, break up, break up for me the old law-tables!"[97] By condemning morality, Nietzsche heralds the advent of nihilism, which has become necessary, for the decadent values that humanity has hith-erto venerated have led it to its decline; hence the need for new values which affirm life and elevate man. However, the nihilism he advocates is an "active nihilism," that is, "nihilism, the sign of increased power of the spirit" which he opposes to passive nihilism, "nihilism, the sign of decadence and regression of spiritual strength."[98] Consequently, his destruction of old values is in itself a creative act, for it aims to establish new and higher values:

> And he who has to be a creator in good and evil, verily he has first to be a destroyer, and break values in pieces. Thus the great evil pertain to the greatest good: that, however, is the creating good.[99]

Nietzsche's active nihilism is in fact a predominant and characteristic trait of his philosophy heralding a superhuman era. He is the godless prophet proclaiming the advent of a superior kind of humanity; but, in order to do so, he must first destroy the very foundations of Western

---

96 Ibid., p. 112.
97 Ibid., p. 250.
98 Friedrich Nietzsche, *The Will to Power*, vol. II, p. 109.
99 Friedrich Nietzsche, *Thus Spoke Zarathustra*, p. 149.

humanist and liberal civilisation, heiress to the Judeo-Christian tradition and its notions of good and evil which have governed humanity for more than two thousand years. Indeed, Nietzsche declares himself the liberator of mankind from the "illusion" called "conscience" or "morality," preaching instead a new moral freedom, or freedom from morality, which only the free spirits can endure.

Active nihilism, for Nietzsche, therefore means the self-overcoming of morality, "morality vanquished by itself," for morality itself—that is, natural morality, characterised by innocence and honesty—obliges us to deny Christian morality, which is hypocritical and anti-natural, a "sacred lie." Yet nihilism is just the first phase in the establishment of new values, of a new philosophy "beyond good and evil"; thus, Nietzsche's *Zarathustra*, who preaches the overcoming of Christianity's concepts of good and evil, represents an attempt to "correct" or transcend the dualism of the historical Zarathustra (the Persian prophet whose vision of the world was based on the eternal conflict between the forces of light and the forces of darkness), a dualism which also formed the basic principle of the Christian religion, one of the main reasons which led Nietzsche to reject Christianity.

The tragic man, the higher man thus rejects the nihilism caused by Christian morality and culminating in the death of God, by adopting the "pessimism of force" and an "active nihilism," that is, by transcending nihilism through a tragic and heroic vision of life, which rejects the "metaphysical consolation," that is, the "redemption in the afterlife," and manifests itself through the sacred Dionysian laughter venerating the existence of a "godless" free spirit:

> Let us picture for ourselves a generation growing up with this fearlessness in its gaze, with this heroic push into what is tremendous; let us picture for ourselves the bold stride of these dragon slayers, the proud audacity with which they turn their backs on all the doctrines of weakness associated with optimism, in order to live with resolution, fully and completely. *Would it not be necessary* that the tragic man of this culture, having trained himself for what is serious and frightening, desire a new art, *the art of metaphysical consolation*, the tragedy, as his own personal Helen of Troy, and to have to cry out with Faust:

> "With my desire's power, should I not call into this life the fairest form of all?" Would it not be necessary? ... No, three times no! You young Romantics: it should not be necessary! But it is very likely that things

will *end up* like that—that you will end up like that—namely, "being consoled," as it stands written, in spite of all the self-training for what is serious and frightening "metaphysically consoled," in short, the way Romantics finish up, as *Christians*... No! You should first learn the art of consolation *in this life*—you should learn to *laugh*, my young friends, even if you wish to remain thoroughly pessimistic. From that, as laughing people, some day or other perhaps you will for once ship all metaphysical consolation to the devil—and then away with metaphysics! Or, to speak the language of that Dionysian fiend called *Zarathustra*:

"Lift up your hearts, my brothers, high, higher! And for my sake don't forget your legs as well! Raise up your legs, you fine dancers, and better yet, stand on your heads!

"This crown of the man who laughs, this crown wreathed with roses—I have placed this crown upon myself. I myself declare my laughter holy. Today I found no one else strong enough for that.

"Zarathustra the dancer, Zarathustra the light-hearted, who beckons with his wings, a man ready to fly, hailing all birds, prepared and ready, a careless and blessed man.

"Zarathustra the truth teller, Zarathustra the true laugher, not an impatient man, not a man of absolutes, someone who loves jumps and leaps to the side—I myself crown myself!

"This crown of the laughing man, this crown of rose wreaths: you my brothers, I throw this crown to you! Laughter I declared sacred: you higher men, for my sake learn—to laugh!"[100]

This passage from *The Birth of Tragedy* perfectly summarises the concept of the "pessimism of strength," of active nihilism advocated by Nietzsche, who "gazes at the abyss with an eagle's eyes" and sacralises the higher laughter, offering his brothers, the "higher men," a "wreath of roses" which symbolises the affirmation of life, the *amor fati*, in contrast to the wreath of thorns of the Crucified, symbol of suffering and death.

This *amor fati*, this pessimism of strength which can only be embraced by the free and higher spirits—those who embody the will to power at its highest level, those who *bear* and *dare to* face truth—this *amor fati* is part of a tragic, heroic philosophy which indeed aims to vanquish

---

100 Friedrich Nietzsche, *The Birth of Tragedy*, pp. 43-44.

the pessimism of weakness and passive nihilism through a "Dionysian affirmation of life":

> How much truth can a spirit bear, how much truth can a spirit *dare?* That has become for me more and more the real measure of value. Error... is not blindness, error is cowardice... Every acquisition, every step forward in knowledge is the result of courage, of severity towards oneself, of cleanliness with respect to oneself... such an experimental philosophy as I live anticipates experimentally even the possibilities of the most fundamental nihilism; but this does not mean that it must halt at a negation, a No, a will to negation. It wants rather to cross over to the opposite of this—to a *Dionysian affirmation* of the world as it is, without subtraction, exception, or selection... the highest state a philosopher can attain: to stand in a Dionysian relationship to existence—my formula for this is *amor fati.*[101]

Thus, the "pessimism" adopted by Nietzsche, far from being a pessimism of weakness—which leads to, and perpetuates an absolute nihilism and a total degeneration of life—on the contrary represents the free, strong, life-affirming spirits who venerate life by ruthlessly destroying all weakness, all notion which is hostile to life; this pessimism of strength therefore perfectly embodies the "nihilism vanquished by itself," and, consequently, represents a "theodicy," a "total affirmation of the world."[102]

Beyond good and evil: The death of Christian morality

By postulating the will to power as the sole reality, as a master morality "beyond good and evil," Nietzschean philosophy logically leads to the following conclusion: "God" and Christian morality are dead, and with them this old illusion of "good and evil." Consequently, without the promise of eternal bliss in an "afterlife" which would be the final goal of life, there can be no "true" or "false," no "good" and "evil," for life has no other purpose but itself; indeed, there are neither "moral actions" nor "immoral actions," there are no opposites, everything is in flux; there are also no "eternal facts" just as there are no "absolute truths."[103]

---

101 Friedrich Nietzsche, *The Will to Power*, vol. II, pp. 274-275.

102 Ibid., p. 303.

103 Friedrich Nietzsche, *Humain, trop Humain (Human, All Too Human)* (Paris: Librairie Générale Française: 1995).

Nothing was created, everything is in eternal becoming. It is only by overcoming morality through the adoption of a philosophy beyond good and evil, beyond the eternal duality between good and evil, between the body and the spirit (a duality which characterises the transcendental vision of the world) that we will be able to restore the innocence of becoming, namely to live in harmony with nature, to affirm life in the pantheistic way in *this* world and in the *present,* to live *for* this world and this present.

Nietzsche's thought was indeed "immanentist," monistic, a belief in human perfection in *this* world, the *real* world, rejecting at the same time—as we have seen in the former chapter—metaphysical transcendentalism (the "will to truth") and hedonistic and sterile materialism (the "will to live"). To Nietzsche, transcendentalism as well as materialism both deny the will to power as a principle of life and as the sole truth which manifests itself in all aspects of existence.

Thus, the actual world is the only real world. Consequently, this world is the only one that has value, for it represents the unique life affirming principle: the will to power.

Nietzsche blames transcendentalism—Platonic and later Christian metaphysics—for the fact that its "will to truth" is a principle that is "hostile to life and destructive," entreating instead the higher men to "remain true to the earth" and not to believe "those who speak to you of superterrestrial hopes" for "they are poisoners... despisers of life!" For Nietzsche, "once blasphemy against God was the greatest blasphemy, but God died, and thereupon these blasphemers died too. To blaspheme the earth is now the most dreadful offence, and to esteem the bowels of the inscrutable more highly than the meaning of the earth."[104]

Nonetheless, as we have demonstrated in the former chapter, Nietzsche's firm condemnation of transcendentalism does not make him a Cartesian rationalist... on the contrary, Nietzsche is just as proud to reject the latter, despising positivism which he blames in his *Genealogy of Morals* for being narrow and superficial, only trusting physical phenomena, material "facts," and only believing in the evidence of the senses as the ultimate source of certainty, thus reducing existence to an unproductive mechanism without any spiritual horizon. Indeed, Nietzsche considers that reason is never the motivation for human action, arguing that facts are only interpretations: "To positivism which only considers

104 Friedrich Nietzsche, *Thus Spoke Zarathustra*, p. 22.

phenomena and says: 'there are only facts' — I would like to object: No, precisely, there are no facts, only interpretations."[105]

Vehemently denouncing the whole rationalist tradition of the Enlightenment and the moral void that it had left behind, Nietzsche despises the liberal-humanist principle of the "will to live" as a simple desire for self-preservation (in contrast to the life affirming principle of the will to power), as an unproductive desire of the common and mediocre "beast-man" who seeks "happiness" instead of power: "for what do the trees in a jungle fight each other? For 'happiness'? For power!"[106]

Power is the very essence of life, the energy that pervades and sustains life. Consequently, the simple desire for survival and search for happiness is nothing but an illusion: "He who shot the doctrine of the 'will to existence' at truth certainly did not hit the truth: this will — does not exist! ... Only where life is, there is also will: not will to life, but — so I teach you — Will to Power!"[107]

Thus, to Nietzsche, reality is monistic, it is neither "good" nor "evil," neither pure spirit nor pure matter, but rather the unity between these different concepts and aspects of life. One should therefore talk about the unity of good and evil, about their inseparability, for they complete each other and are an integral part of the will to power: "supreme good and supreme evil are identical... man must grow better and more evil... the most evil is necessary for the superman's best,"[108] says Nietzsche, for, to him, "evil" guarantees strength,[109] which is the only criterion of a full and creative life (which "good" is not). Insisting on the organic and fundamental unity of nature as a whole, Nietzsche's philosophy is holistic, rejecting all separation between the body and the spirit, perfection being symbolised by the union between the Apollonian and Dionysian spirits which incarnate respectively reason and the irrational.

"A healthy mind in a healthy body" — nowhere else does this axiom find more significance than in Nietzsche's philosophy. Indeed, Nietzsche despises the Christian notion of the intrinsic superiority of the spirit over the body, and the soul which "looks at the body with contempt"; he also despises the "weak and sickly" body which pretends to possess a

105 Friedrich Nietzsche, *The Will to Power*, vol. I, p. 265.

106 Ibid., vol. II, p. 149.

107 Friedrich Nietzsche, *Thus Spoke Zarathustra*, pp. 148-149.

108 Friedrich Nietzsche, *The Will to Power*, vol. II, pp. 414, 443.

109 "That the nature of man is evil, is my consolation: it guarantees 'strength'!" Ibid., p. 417.

"sublime soul." To Nietzsche, true perfection is both spiritual and physical, health being physiological as well as moral.

Becoming and "eternal recurrence": The will to power's creative evolution

With the concept of eternal recurrence, we find another characteristic trait of Nietzsche's philosophy, a concept that reminds us of the Hindu-inspired theosophical theory of reincarnation and evolutionary cycles. To Nietzsche, "everything goes, everything returns; eternally rolls the wheel of existence. Everything dies, everything blossoms anew; the year of existence runs on forever... the middle is everywhere. Crooked is the path of eternity."[110]

In *Beyond Good and Evil*, Nietzsche explains how energy is not unlimited, and how, consequently, it is eternally active; however, as it cannot eternally create new forms, it must repeat itself, hence the "eternal recurrence" of all things. To "being," or static truth, Nietzsche opposes "becoming," a dynamic process, eternally changing, eternally creative, a perpetual elevation and overcoming, without beginning or end, without a final goal. That, to Nietzsche, is the very essence of life, the dynamic of existence, the motor of history. Nietzsche adopts Heraclitus' famous phrase "everything is in flux"; everything is in perpetual motion, the world is endlessly becoming, thus the search for a final goal and eternal peace, the teleological metaphysicians' concept of "being" is an illusion.

The concept of becoming, represented by the Nietzschean doctrine of eternal recurrence, is in fact but one of the manifestations of the will to power, as Nietzsche's following description of the "world" illustrates:

> And do you know what "the world" is to me? Shall I show it to you in my mirror? This world: a monster of energy, without beginning, without end; a firm, iron magnitude of force that does not grow bigger or smaller, that does not expend itself but only transforms itself; as a whole, of unalterable size, a household without expenses or losses, but likewise without increase or income; enclosed by "nothingness" as by a boundary; not something blurry or wasted, not something endlessly extended, but set in a definite space as a definite force, and not a sphere that might be "empty" here or there, but rather as force throughout, as a play of forces and waves of forces, at the same time one and many, increasing

---

110 Friedrich Nietzsche, *Thus Spoke Zarathustra*, p. 269.

here and at the same time decreasing there; a sea of forces flowing and rushing together, eternally changing, eternally flooding back, with tremendous years of recurrence, with an ebb and a flood of its forms; out of the simplest forms striving toward the most complex, out of the stillest, most rigid, coldest forms toward the hottest, most turbulent, most self-contradictory, and then again returning home to the simple out of this abundance, out of the play of contradictions back to the joy of concord, still affirming itself in this uniformity of its courses and its years, blessing itself as that which must return eternally, as a becoming that knows no satiety, no disgust, no weariness: this, my Dionysian world of the eternally self-creating, the eternally self-destroying, this mystery world of the twofold voluptuous delight, my "beyond good and evil," without goal, unless the joy of the circle is itself a goal; without will, unless a ring feels good will toward itself—do you want a name for this world? A solution for all its riddles? A light for you, too, you best-concealed, strongest, most intrepid, most midnightly men? This world is the will to power--and nothing besides! And you yourselves are also this will to power—and nothing besides![111]

"Immoralism" as a transvaluation of values and restoration of the natural order

As we have already demonstrated, Nietzsche considers that Christianity represents an inversion of ancient values, a slave morality which, by inventing a "beyond" as unique salvation for man, has led to the denial of life, of the real world, and has held mankind in moral and intellectual bondage for millennia. The result is the actual rule of nihilism caused by the victory of the values of the slave (the Christian) over the values of the free and strong spirit (the pagan).

Consequently, Nietzsche strives to restore the natural order of rank, the pyramid of life, by undertaking a new inversion- or "transvaluation"—of values, thereby advocating a return to the ancient pagan aristocratic, life-affirming values in order to replace Christian "herd" values; therein lies the significance of his "immoralism," which is *not*, as is widely perceived, an absolute or destructive nihilism, rather a return to the "innocence of becoming," the state of nature.

To Nietzsche, the causes of nihilism are mainly the absence of superior types and the "tyranny" of the masses and herd values:

---

111 Friedrich Nietzsche, *The Will to Power*, vol. I, pp. 235-236.

Causes of nihilism:

1. The absence of a superior race, namely that whose fertility and inexhaustible power maintain faith in mankind...

2. The inferior species (the "herd," the "mob," "society") unlearns modesty and amplifies its needs to the extent of attributing to them a cosmic and metaphysical value. All of existence thus becomes vulgar: indeed, given that it is the mob which rules, it tyrannises exceptions who lose faith in themselves and become nihilists. All attempts at inventing higher types fail... the result: resistance to higher types. Decadence and uncertainty of all higher types. Struggle against the genius (popular poetry, etc.). Pity for the humble and the suffering, taken to be the measure of the elevation of the soul. What lacks is the philosopher who interprets action instead of translating it into poetry.[112]

Morality in itself is not a reprehensible thing. Indeed, there are two kinds of morality, and they are "not to be confused," says Nietzsche:

That which defends itself against emerging decadence with the help of an instinct which has remained healthy, and that which, precisely serving this decadence to formulate itself, justify itself, is in itself a cause of decline. The first is usually stoic, tough, tyrannical (stoicism was one of these moralities destined to halt); the other is exalted, sentimental, full of mysteries, it belongs to women and "beautiful sentiments" (primitive Christianity was one of those morals).[113]

"There they stand before me... they laugh; they do not hear me; I am not the mouth for these ears":[114] the greatest error made by Nietzsche's Zarathustra was that he started preaching his radically aristocratic philosophy, his free thought "beyond good and evil," to the populace of the market place, an inferior type of man who was incapable of understanding such deep thoughts destined for lofty souls.

Consequently, following his initial disappointment in mankind, Zarathustra resolved hitherto to preach his highest teachings to the "very rare," to the exceptions, namely the higher men who have the courage to accept the true essence and only goal of life: the will to power. Truth, for

---

112 Ibid., vol. II, pp. 34-35.
113 Ibid., vol. I, p. 147.
114 Friedrich Nietzsche, *Thus Spoke Zarathustra*, p. 26.

Nietzsche, is essentially a question of courage, and only the exceptional beings can bear and dare to face reality (the "abyss" or the "mirror") and to live in conformity with nature's aristocratic law of selection.

Indeed, all aristocratic, hierarchical civilisations distinguish between exoteric, common knowledge available to all men, and esoteric, exclusive knowledge reserved for the rare few, the initiates. As Nietzsche always reminds us, Zarathustra's wise and deep words are not destined for those with "long ears" (the asses), the ignorant mob which is unworthy of such truths:

> It is inevitable, it is even right, that our supreme insights must—and should!—sound like follies, in certain cases like crimes, when they come impermissible to the ears of those who are not predisposed and predestined for them. The exoteric and the esoteric as philosophers formerly distinguished them, among the Indians as among the Greeks, Persians and Moslems, in short wherever one believed in an order of rank and not in equality and equal rights.[115]

The logical conclusion that Nietzsche draws from this unbridgeable gulf between minority and majority, between the exceptions and the "many-too-many," is the following: mankind is not "one," as humanists—Christians and secularists alike—pretend; rather, it is divided into two distinct and unequal "species," the (rare) masters (the creators, the free spirits, the strong and lofty souls, such as the Greeks and Romans) and the (many) "slaves" (the weak, the suffering and the unproductive herd types embodied by the Christian and the Jew). Consequently, morality and justice are neither universal nor absolute.

Thus, Nietzsche thinks, one must not talk of universal virtues and values, for to each type of man—the master and the slave—there is a different morality; that is the natural order of things, the natural order of rank. Nietzschean morality—in contrast to Christian morality—is thus "the theory of hierarchy between men and consequently also of the value of their acts and their works in line according to this hierarchy; it is thus the theory of human value judgments."[116] Hence, to each caste its own morality.

Indeed, Nietzsche is clear in his rejection of the notion that *all* men have a moral dignity, moral worth, and moral rights. To Nietzsche, true

---

115 Friedrich Nietzsche, *Beyond Good and Evil*, p. 48.
116 Friedrich Nietzsche, *The Will to Power*, vol. II, p. 143.

justice is unequal, given that those who lack noble souls cannot rise above mediocrity. Hence his slogan "become who you are" only applies to exceptional beings. Consequently, Nietzsche declares that "he has discovered himself who says: This is my good and my evil. He has thus silenced the mole and dwarf who says: 'Good for all, evil for all.'"[117]

Given that justice and morality are not universal, therefore, there is a hierarchy of values, as well as two different—even antithetical—moralities that Nietzsche calls "master morality" and "slave morality," the former being characterized by pride, honour, and glory, the latter by cowardice, envy, and resentment. Nietzsche's aristocratic vision of the world thus divides mankind into superhuman "masters" and subhuman "slaves," each of these classes or species having their own table of values. To Nietzsche, the master considers the antithesis "good" and "bad" as identical to "noble" and "contemptible," the antithesis "good" and "evil" having its origin elsewhere:

> Evil actions belong to the powerful and virtuous; bad, base ones to the subjected. The most powerful man, the creator, should be the most evil, in as much as he makes prevalent in other men his ideal against their ideal and transforms them in his image. Evil means tough, painful, imposed.[118]

Nietzsche's master morality may be summarised as follows:

> The cowardly, the timid, the petty, and those who think only of narrow utility are despised... The noble type of man feels himself to be the determiner of values... he creates values. Everything he knows to be part of himself, he honours: such a morality is self-glorification. In the foreground stands the feeling of plenitude, of power which seeks to overflow, the happiness of high tension, the consciousness of a wealth which would like to give away and bestow—the noble human being too aids the unfortunate but not, or almost not, from pity, but from an urge begotten by superfluity of power.[119]

Despising the Christian "slavish" virtues of the "warm heart," "selflessness," and "abnegation," the master exhibits an inborn dignity of high

117 Friedrich Nietzsche, *Thus Spoke Zarathustra*, p. 242.
118 Friedrich Nietzsche, *The Will to Power*, vol. II, p. 338.
119 Friedrich Nietzsche, *Beyond Good and Evil*, pp. 214-215.

rank and a reverence for the past and for tradition, coupled with contempt for "modern" egalitarian ideas of "progress."

This highly aristocratic morality justifies arbitrary and even ruthless conduct towards those who are inferior of spirit and character, but, on the other hand, it considers that one has a duty towards one's peers; in other words, equality, duty and loyalty exist only *inter pares* ("among equals"), i.e. among aristocrats, the noble of soul and spirit. Indeed, Nietzsche is firmly convinced that the true slogan of justice is to be "equal to the equal" and "unequal to the unequal."

As we have already seen in the first chapter, in contrast to the master morality, the slave morality is a creation of the resentment of the weak, the miserable, the sickly, against the strong, healthy, aristocratic types. It builds its antithetical values of "good and evil" in reaction to the master's antinomy "good and bad"; it considers the noble's notion of "good" as "evil," whilst adopting the master's concept of "bad" as its supreme "good". Nietzsche thus highlights the main characteristics of this decadent morality, the morality of the "abused, oppressed, suffering, unfree, those uncertain of themselves and weary":

> [A] pessimistic mistrust of the entire situation of man... The slave is suspicious of the virtues of the powerful: he is sceptical and mistrustful, keenly mistrustful, of everything "good" that is honoured among them... On the other hand... pity, the kind and helping hand, the warm heart, patience, industriousness, humility, friendliness come into honour... Slave morality is essentially the morality of utility. Here is the source of the famous antithesis "good" and "evil" — power and danger were felt to exist in evil... Thus, according to slave morality the "evil" inspire fear; according to master morality it is precisely the "good" who inspire fear and want to inspire it, while the "bad" man is judged contemptible... Wherever slave morality comes to predominate, language exhibits a tendency to bring the words "good" and "stupid" closer to each other.[120]

In the *Genealogy of Morals*, Nietzsche traces the origin of the Christian antinomy "good and evil" which he opposes to the ancient, Roman antinomy "good and bad." Indeed, according to Nietzsche, the conflict between master morality and slave morality is best represented by the opposition between the two antagonisms "good and bad" and "good

---

120 Ibid., pp. 216-217.

and evil," i.e. respectively the aristocratic and "immoral"—or rather supra-moral—values of the strong, the masters, against the plebeian, base values of the weak, the slaves.

Thus, Nietzsche considers that the Christian antinomy "good and evil," which embodies the morality of the slave, builds its notions of good and evil only in reaction to—and in opposition to—the master morality (which creates values) and its notions of "good" and "bad"; consequently, what the master considers as "bad" becomes the slave's "good," and what represents the good for the master becomes the slave's "bad." These two moralities remain forever irreconcilable, given that they derive from two different visions of life, representing two types of humanity, two distinct species.

Nietzsche, in his *Genealogy of Morals*, considered that the historical conflict between Rome and Judea perfectly represented the existential and spiritual opposition between master and slave morality, between the strong, aristocratic, natural values of the pagans (Romans, Greeks, etc.) and the weak, servile, anti-natural values of the Jews; in other words, "Rome against Judea"—as Nietzsche wrote—symbolised the eternal struggle between the antinomies "good and bad" and "good and evil."

The conflict between the ancient, pagan, natural world and the modern anti-pagan, Judeo-Christian world thus summarises the spiritual and moral war which opposed, for millennia, the pre-Christian "masters" and the Judeo-Christian "slaves"; this "war of the spirits" goes on till this day through the opposition between the free, anti-modern spirits who adopt an "immoralism" and an atheism *à la* Nietzsche and despise "progress," that is, "equal rights for all," which they consider as a levelling—i.e. a "mediocrisation"—of society (to use Nietzsche's term), and those who declare themselves Judeo-Christians (or, in case they are secular, "liberals"); today these are the modern, egalitarian "humanists," the so-called "free thinkers" whom Nietzsche considers as "fake free spirits," those who preach a hedonistic freedom empty of meaning and purpose ("free *for* what?" asked Zarathustra).

Thus, this is an eternal struggle between healthy, aristocratic, natural paganism and Judeo-Christianity, this anti-natural movement which incarnates "sick" values and weariness of life, thereby confirming Nietzsche's affirmation that there exists a vast chasm between the lofty free spirits, and the weak, herd-like and mediocre "little men," a chasm that is so deep that it pushes us to distinguish between two different species which will remain eternally irreconcilable and at war with each other.

Given the fact that we are now living in the "era of the slave" brought about by the victory of slave morality, i.e. the "universalisation" of the levelling, mediocre, egalitarian values of Christian morality (or its secularised modern version, liberal democracy), and given the fact that the distinction between the existing standards of "good" and "evil" is wholly man-made (each class creating its own values, which are antithetical), it follows that the only way to restore human greatness and to overcome the "human, all too human" is through the inversion of the actually prevalent notions of "good" and "evil," for they represent the slave's decadent version of the "lie which has hitherto been called truth."

Therefore, after advocating "active nihilism" as a destructive but liberating philosophy "beyond good and evil," Nietzsche proceeds to preach a "transvaluation of values," what he calls "immoralism," that is, a return to the master morality, to the aristocratic values and notions of "good and bad" which were prevalent among the ancient Romans and Greeks, a strong, proud and noble species of man.

"The good and just call me the destroyer of morals: my story is immoral":[121] Nietzsche's "immoralism" is the free spirits' war against the old values, an affirmative call for a spiritual awakening confirmed by his assertion that denial and destruction is a condition of affirmation and is therefore not to be confused with the anarchist's "amoralism" (absence of values) or "passive nihilism," i.e. the destruction of the old law-tables without creating values anew. "Evil in the service of the (real) good" was indeed a favourite Nietzschean slogan, for he thought the following:

When a decadence-species of man has risen to the rank of the highest species of man, this can happen only at the expense of its antithetical species, the species of man strong and certain of life. When the herd-animal is resplendent in the glow of the highest virtue, the exceptional man must be devalued to the wicked man. When mendaciousness at any price appropriates the word "truth" for its perspective, what is actually veracious must be discovered bearing the worst names.[122]

---

121 Friedrich Nietzsche, *Thus Spoke Zarathustra*, p. 90.
122 Friedrich Nietzsche, *Ecce Homo*, p. 191.

Therefore, the only way to restore the aristocrat's "good" is to fight against the slave's "good," i.e. to become "evil"; Nietzsche thus wonders in *Human, All Too Human* whether it would be possible to "invert all values," given that it is precisely the "good" which represents "evil."

Hence, for Nietzsche, what is "good" is everything that proceeds from—and increases—power, and what is "bad" is everything that is weak; therefore, an action acquires its value not depending on whether it is intrinsically "good" or "evil," but on whether or not it guarantees and increases power, and hence leads to spiritual progress, to the self-overcoming of the human species. And history shows that great cultures have mostly arisen by means of powerful and "immoral" actions, which are the highest manifestation of the principle of will to power inherent in nature.

Consequently, the great epochs of our life are the occasions when we gain the courage to rebaptise our "evil" qualities as our best qualities: "man must grow better and more evil," teaches Nietzsche, for "the most evil is necessary to the Superman's strength."[123] This Nietzschean famous affirmation celebrates and encapsulates on its own the will to power as a philosophy "beyond good and evil."

To use force, to exploit the weak, to deny morality, thus becomes permissible for the higher man, for—as Nietzsche says—"when nothing is true, everything is permitted"; or, as he explains in his *Genealogy of Morals*, he who can command, he who is a born master, he who comes on the scene forceful in deed and gesture, he who justifies human existence itself—what has he to do with morals?

According to Nietzsche, "immoralism," put in the service of the Superman, is not only justified and permitted, but in fact desired; thus spoke Nietzsche, the immoralist: "Jesus said to his Jews: 'The law was made for servants—love God as I love him, as his son! What have we sons of God to do with morality!'"[124]

123 Friedrich Nietzsche, *Thus Spoke Zarathustra*, p. 349.
124 Friedrich Nietzsche, *Beyond Good and Evil*, p. 103.

-II- The will to power as self-overcoming: The new nobility, prelude to the Superman

To Nietzsche, self-overcoming, and hence the overcoming of man as a species, constitutes the supreme goal of life and the noblest manifestation of the will to power: "Life itself told me this secret: 'behold,' it said, 'I am that which must overcome itself again and again.'"[125]

Eternal self-overcoming, which culminates in the creation of the *Übermensch*, the Superman, is thus the very essence of life. Nietzsche writes in *The Will to Power*: "It lies within our nature to create a being higher than ourselves. To create beyond ourselves! That is what drives us to procreate."[126] Indeed, Nietzsche teaches us that "man is the animal whose nature has not yet been fixed,"[127] and so man is a bridge, not a goal.

Life as such—that is, the will to power—is a process of eternal creation, of perpetual overcoming; a process which transcends mere self-preservation and self-mastery to include man's actual sacrifice in order to create something higher than him, the Superman. Indeed, in contrast to the liberal and humanist conception of man, Nietzsche considers that nature's and life's aristocratic law is not mere self-preservation, but self-domination and self-overcoming; instead of the liberal question "how shall man be preserved?", Nietzsche asks the question "how shall man be overcome?"

Self-overcoming first involves self-mastery: men are classified according to their ability to control and master their own weaknesses and desires, and therefore to be the masters, not the slaves, of their instincts, in what Nietzsche calls "the innocence of the senses." The strongest and most spiritual men, according to Nietzsche, find their happiness where others would find their destruction: in the "labyrinth," in hardness towards themselves and others, in self-conquest.

An ascetic "happiness" of that kind, which consists in mastering—and not repressing—the senses (nonetheless without falling into beastly hedonism) is the distinctive sign of higher beings who live dangerously and experiment:

---

125 Friedrich Nietzsche, *Thus Spoke Zarathustra*, p. 148.

126 Friedrich Nietzsche, *The Will to Power*, vol. II, p. 362.

127 Friedrich Nietzsche, *Beyond Good and Evil*, p. 82.

The higher caste, being perfect... owes it to itself to maintain this sort of happiness which is bought at the cost of absolute obedience towards oneself and which consists of imposing upon oneself all sorts of austerity, of self-mastery and rigor; it wants us to recognise in it the species of men which is the most worthy of veneration, but also of admiration; thus it cannot accommodate itself of just any kind of happiness.[128]

Towards a new synthetic aristocracy

According to Nietzsche, a higher species of men must eventually distinguish itself from the amorphous mass and rule over the earth so that self-overcoming, which represents the noblest manifestation of the will to power and the law of nature, culminates in the creation of the Superman, supreme goal of mankind (a concept that will be discussed in the third chapter). It is from this "new nobility," as Nietzsche calls it, that the Superman shall emerge; it is thus the prelude to the new superhuman dawn of mankind, the "bridge" towards the Superman.

It is worth noting that when Nietzsche talks about the "masters" and the "aristocrats," it is mainly and essentially in a philosophical and spiritual sense, rather than in a traditional or historic sense: the new nobility of "higher men," destined to create the Superman, is an aristocracy based on the greatness of soul and spirit, a "synthetic" aristocracy of "complete" or "whole" men who justify existence and prepare the advent of the Superman, in contrast to the "fragmentary men" who form the vegetating majority of humanity:

> The majority of men are a fragmentary and exclusive image of man: one must add them up to obtain a man. Entire epochs, entire peoples have in this sense something that is fragmentary; it may be necessary to the growth of man that he only develops bit by bit. Thus one must not ignore that basically, the real issue is the production of the synthetic man; lower men, the tremendous majority, are merely preludes and rehearsals out of whose medley the whole man appears here and there, the milestone man who indicates how far humanity has advanced so far.[129]

---

128 Friedrich Nietzsche, *The Will to Power*, vol. II, p. 380.
129 Ibid., p. 415.

In contrast to the "weakening" and "mediocrisation" of humanity, Nietzsche believes that "an opposite movement is necessary, which produces the synthetic man, the totalising, justifying man, he whose existence demands this mechanisation of humanity, for it is on this basis that he could invent and build his higher form of existence. He needs the *hostility* of the mob, of the 'levelled' men, of the feeling of his distance towards them; he is established on them, he is nourished by them. This higher form of aristocracy is the future's."[130]

The superiority of the members of this synthetic aristocracy resides not merely in their physical force, but mainly in their psychic force, for they are "complete human beings," as Nietzsche says, he who believes in a nobility "in moral questions also." The "whole" man, for Nietzsche, is a man who incarnates the supreme degree of will to power, which is none other than the degree of courage, the degree of the endurance of reality, of truth, and the refusal to invent another life as an escape from the suffering and cruelty of our world. That is how the "synthetic nobility" of "whole" individuals represents "the union of spiritual superiority and the well-being and excess of power," as Nietzsche describes it in *Beyond Good and Evil*.

Nietzsche therefore speaks of an aristocracy based on innate genius, and not a traditional aristocracy based on heredity, titles or possessions. When Nietzsche mentions the "higher men," the new aristocracy, the "lords of the earth," the "master race," he talks about a *race* of higher men — the word "race" is used here in the sense of a universal higher caste, a superhuman species which is yet unborn, which must be born, and not in the conventional sense — he talks about a species which forms itself in opposition to the predominant herd type: "I write for a race of men that does not exist yet, for the 'masters of the earth.'"[131]

This "coming" higher caste reminds us of the Greeks and Romans of antiquity who, according to Nietzsche, were part of such a healthy and strong race; but it no longer exists in our age of universal suffrage, thus it belongs to the distant past as well as to the future, and not to the Christian or modern era, for it could not be born out of mediocre, egalitarian, levelling modernity, nor from what Nietzsche calls "bovine nationalism," for this race of masters represents isolated and solitary men of exception:

---

130 Ibid., p. 419.
131 Ibid., p. 402.

It is a comfort to me to know that above the steam and filth of human lowlands there is a higher, brighter humanity, very small in number (for everything outstanding is by its nature rare); one belongs to it, not because one is more talented or more virtuous or more heroic or more loving than the men below, but because one is colder, brighter, more far-seeing, more solitary; because one endures, prefers, demands solitude as happiness, as privilege, indeed as a condition of existence.[132]

Thus, Nietzsche keeps hoping that this dispersed humanity, "separated" and solitary, will one day form a *race,* a *people,* and will rule over the earth in order to enable the advent of the Superman that it shall breed:

You solitaries of today, you who have seceded from society, you shall one day be a people: from you, who have chosen out yourselves, shall a chosen people spring—and from this chosen people, the Superman.[133]

It is this new aristocracy, this synthetic nobility of the future that would pave the way for the Superman, who incarnates the overcoming of man by man, the apex of the will to power, following the self-overcoming of morality or "nihilism vanquished by itself." Arch-enemy of the reign of the comfort and mediocrity so characteristic of modernity, Nietzsche rejected all "old law-tables," condemning the "slave ideology" that is Christianity, and advocating instead a radically elitist philosophy and vision of the world: "aristocratic radicalism," a doctrine unique in the fact that it represents a "third way" between corrupt egalitarian democracy and the materialist and levelling socialism of the mob, while distinguishing itself from "bovine nationalism" as well as traditional aristocratic conservatism through its advocacy of the notion of a "new nobility" of Platonic inspiration.

This new nobility shall be based not on ownership of wealth, property, or inherited titles that one neither deserves nor is worthy of (as the corrupt traditional aristocracy of the past two centuries); it shall rather be based on the superiority of the soul, spirit, and the degree of psychic power, and thus on merit and real superiority characteristic of a strong race of men, of the aristocrats of antiquity, who to this day represent the only real aristocrats.

---

132 Ibid., pp. 436-437.
133 Friedrich Nietzsche, *Thus Spoke Zarathustra*, p. 102.

In other words, the nobility that Nietzsche dreams of is based on the will to power—the latter being essentially represented by self-overcoming, courage, the endurance of truth, mental, moral, and psychic force and superiority, a healthy body and a strong, authentic character. Indeed, Nietzsche strove to reestablish, in an age of *"universal suffrage,"* the order of rank as order of power, a natural order in which what determines rank is the quantity of power that we are, the rest being "cowardice."

Real justice is the will of the strongest, namely the strongest in character, the best, he who endures the most, the creator with the highest spirituality, the freest man who needs neither God nor morality, the man who wants to overcome himself and become divine.

Nietzsche believed that no human excellence, greatness, creativity and nobility were possible except in aristocratic societies, whose members possessed, to a high degree, the "will to dominate" arising out of *megalothymia*, which is the desire to be recognised as better than the others, a characteristic feature of all societies which believe in the spiritual hierarchy of the order of rank and in the inequality between men.

To Nietzsche, aristocracy represents the natural order and the supreme law of life; consequently, he advocated the reestablishment of Brahmanism's ancient Indo-European order of castes based on the code of Manu, a system whose social hierarchy was based on spiritual superiority, a system that should serve as a model for the politics of the future:

> The order of castes, the supreme, the dominating law, is only the sanctioning of a natural order, a natural law of the first rank... Nature... separates from one another the predominantly spiritual type, the predominantly muscular and temperamental type, and the mediocre type—the last as the great majority, the first as the elite... the order of castes, order of rank, only formulates the supreme law of life itself.[134]

The order of castes thus incarnates the natural law of hierarchy. Men are radically unequal; consequently, the strongest and most gifted in spirit and in intellect, must rule over the majority of under-gifted and unproductive beings. Any attempt to impose equality is thus considered as immoral, for inequality is justice itself; thus spoke Nietzsche:

---

134 Friedrich Nietzsche, *The Will to Power*, vol. I, p. 407.

For justice speaks thus to me: "men are not equal." And they should not
become so, either! Indeed, what would my love for the Superman be, if
I spoke differently?[135]

Only a synthetic aristocracy can achieve human greatness and create the
Superman, whereas liberal democracy's materialist egalitarianism only
leads to mediocrity. A characteristic feature of Nietzsche's "aristocratic
radicalism" is therefore his call for the creation of a "new nobility," a
community of higher men who represent the "bridge" leading to the
Superman, a nobility which would replace the outdated traditional aristocracy, based on heredity, as well as the "money aristocracy."

According to Nietzsche, only an aristocracy of a different nature
could restore greatness in this decaying world: "Therefore, O my brothers," wrote Nietzsche, "is a new nobility needed: to oppose all mob-rule
and all despotism and to write anew upon new law-tables the word:
'noble.' For many noblemen are needed, and noblemen of many kinds,
for nobility to exist! Or, as I once said in a parable: 'precisely this is godliness, that there are gods but no God!'"[136]

Why a "new" nobility? What does Nietzsche reproach the old aristocracy—traditional aristocracy—or the "aristocracy" of money, the
actual financial elite? Staunch opponent of all materialism, Nietzsche
believed that true superiority is never based on wealth, for the latter is
only something we *possess*, not something we *are*. Therefore, the money
aristocracy or oligarchy which prevails in our times is a fake elite which
is only distinguished from the social "lower classes" by virtue of its possessions, not by virtue of its inherent spiritual or moral worth, as was the
case in antiquity, more particularly in Brahmanic India, where the social
hierarchy was based on true superiority, which is always spiritual, never
material.

As regards traditional aristocracy, Nietzsche—totally in line with
the aristocratic radicalism which he advocates, and despite the fact that
he is sometimes wrongly classified as a "neo-aristocratic conservative"
(whereas he was delighted by the description of his philosophy as "aristocratic radicalism")—Nietzsche also criticises the conservatives (his
philosophising "with a hammer" sparing no one), arguing that, granted
that tradition was to be revered and respected, it was nonetheless and

---

135 Friedrich Nietzsche, *Thus Spoke Zarathustra*, p. 130.
136 Ibid., p. 252.

henceforth neither possible nor even desirable to restore the virtues of the past which, on their own, would not be able—and would not suffice—to bring the aristocrats back to power: "the aristocrats of the past, whether ecclesiastic or civilian, prove nothing against the necessity of a new aristocracy."[137]

Moreover, Nietzsche underlines the necessity of a nobility which looks to the future, and not the past; thus, he foresees a "coming" nobility which forges its way towards the higher spheres of social hierarchy through its *own* struggle, its *own* merit. The aristocracy and monarchy of the past must therefore be replaced by the "higher men," the "lords of the earth," who are even higher than kings:

> The age of kings is past: what today calls itself the people deserves no king... what do kings matter any longer! ... We are on our way to find the higher man—the man who is higher than we: although we are kings, for the highest man should also be the highest lord on earth.[138]

Nietzsche thus talks about a new nobility:

> Verily, not a nobility that you could buy like shopkeepers with shopkeepers' gold; for little worth is all that has its price. Not where you come from shall constitute your honour from now on, but instead where you are going! Your will and your foot, which wants to go over and beyond yourself—let that constitute your new honour! Certainly not that you served—what do princes matter anymore! Or that you became a bulwark for what stands, to make it to stand more firmly! Not that your kinfolk became courtiers at courts, and learned to stand long hours like a colourful flamingo in shallow ponds. For *being able* to stand is a merit among courtiers; and all courtiers believe that part of the blessedness after death is— *being allowed* to sit![139]

True superiority being spiritual, and hence *inborn,* not material—linked to the socio-economic status based on *acquired* titles or possessions—it follows that the new aristocrats, for Nietzsche, are separated and isolated individuals who can be born just as well among the rich or the poor. The socio-economic status has nothing to do with real superiority—and

137 Friedrich Nietzsche, *The Will to Power*, vol. II, p. 372.
138 Friedrich Nietzsche, *Thus Spoke Zarathustra*, p. 299.
139 Ibid., p. 253.

thus natural nobility—which is essentially represented by the greatness of the soul, and not wealth or pompous titles.

The "little word" *von*, that is, the simple noble title which is inherited—or bought nowadays "as with the shopkeepers"—does not count anymore as a criterion of nobility for Nietzsche, who specifies that when he defends the idea that "there is only nobility of birth, nobility of blood," he is not speaking here of the "little word" (*von*), "or of the *Almanach de Gotha*," in his "parenthesis for asses,"[140] those superficial conservatives defending traditional aristocracy.

The new aristocracy shall be an aristocracy of the spirit (that is, neither traditional, nor a simple "intellectual aristocracy"), a synthetic nobility of complete men, "aristocrats without a title," *natural* aristocrats belonging to the "master race," a universal race of higher men, the only real lords of the earth, "the first aristocrats in the history of the spirit" whose pride consists in having "an ascendance" and not a descent.[141]

The "aristocratic radicalism" advocated by Nietzsche is thus clearly not an apology for aristocratic conservatism, let alone the rule of the rich or the powerful of the moment; contrary to the financial "elite" and the political "elite"—or other so-called "elites"—of our times, the nobility of the future will be a natural and spiritual aristocracy of "born masters."

Even when Nietzsche declares that "spirit alone does not make noble; rather, there should be something to ennoble the spirit. What is then required? Blood,"[142] thus admitting that "blood" is an attribute of superiority which is as essential as spirit, he is certainly not using this term ("blood") in the social sense (i.e. traditional hereditary aristocracy), or in a narrow racial sense. Rather, he means that "blood" represents the innate and individual superiority of the *natural* aristocrat (who is not *necessarily* an actual aristocrat), and not a social or racial privilege which is automatically transmitted—without any merit—from generation to generation (and represented respectively by the little word *von* and belonging to a certain race).

"Blood," for Nietzsche, has nothing to do with social status or racial heredity, neither is it the product of education or the environment. It is essentially an *internal*, psychic concept, which denotes individual

---

140 Friedrich Nietzsche, *The Will to Power*, vol. II, p. 367.
141 Ibid., p. 462.
142 Ibid., p. 367.

superiority of the exceptional being, the whole man with a higher body and spirit.

Nietzsche considers that the order of rank is not a question of (racial or social) heredity but a question of creativity, of overflowing energy, of psychic, moral, and intellectual higher power, a question of caste, of inequality, of toughness, of endurance, of courage, of stoicism, of absolute will to power characterising the "future lords of the earth," the true free spirits:

> We... who have opened our eyes and our conscience to the question where and how the plant "man" has hitherto grown up most vigorously, we think that this has always happened under the opposite conditions (of those of herd morality), that the perilousness of his situation had first to become tremendous, his powers of invention and dissimulation (his "spirit") had, under protracted pressure and constraint, to evolve into subtlety and daring, his will to life had to be intensified into unconditional will to power—we think that severity, force, slavery, peril in the street and in the heart, concealment, stoicism... serves to enhance the species "man," in contrast to herd desiderata. A morality which has these paradoxical aims, which wants to elevate man instead of debasing him to a useful and mediocre level, a morality which aims to select a dominant caste—that of the future *lords of the earth*—must... before all select a new race in which the same will, the same instinct, will be guaranteed to last for several generations: a new race, a new caste of masters... to prepare a *transvaluation of values* for a vigorous and well defined human race endowed with the highest intellect and the greatest energy... whoever has thought of this program is one of us, is a free spirit, but of a different kind than those who have hitherto called themselves free thinkers: for those wanted approximately the opposite.[143]

The so-called "free thinkers" are very different from the free spirits and therefore "not among us," says Nietzsche, adding: "no, sirs: you want approximately the opposite of what these philosophers whom I call 'tempters' want; those do not feel tempted to exchange with you deceitful politeness. Moreover, if you 'free thinkers' had a hint of what we want to free ourselves from and the direction which we will then take! I think that then you would become the staunchest enemies of what I call my 'freedom of spirit' and my position 'beyond good and evil.'"[144]

143 Ibid., pp. 272-273.
144 Ibid., p.148.

Anyway, there are *no* free spirits in the modern world: "Where are the free spirits nowadays? Show me one free spirit today!"[145]

Nietzsche believes that true genius is innate, never acquired; he thus declares himself "*against* the doctrine of the influence of the milieu and external causes: the force within is infinitely superior; much that looks like external influence is merely its adaptation from within. The same environments could be interpreted and exploited in opposite manner; there are no facts—a genius is not explained in terms of such conditions of his origin."[146]

One is *born* superior; one does not *become* superior; however, this superiority must be proven—through creativity and a tragic attitude towards life (in contrast to the Christian attitude)—in order to be earned and consequently imposed in a Nietzschean hierarchy which is none other than a meritocracy.

Thus, in the "new aristocracy" advocated by Nietzsche, it is "blood" (i.e. the *individual* physiological, psychic and spiritual makeup, not that of a social or racial group *grosso modo*) which determines social rank; it is therefore a hierarchy based on true superiority, *innate* superiority (which is both spiritual and biological, in the sense of a healthy body and mind), and not a fake superiority based on *acquired* privileges such as inherited titles and properties. In short, it is a "native aristocracy," for, to Nietzsche, "an *instinctive* manner of acting and judging is the sign of a good race; to gnaw at oneself and dissect oneself is base."[147]

This new aristocracy will be an aristocracy that eternally renews itself—not through heredity, rather through individual greatness that only a meritocracy can discover and incorporate in a hierarchical order—an "aristocracy of the body and the spirit, which selects itself, perpetually encompasses new elements and distinguishes itself from the democratic world of weak and incomplete men."[148]

The order of rank, or natural hierarchy, is the order of life, the natural order; men are not equal nor shall they ever become equal, whatever the degree of levelling that democracy imposes on them: that is the supreme truth sanctified by nature itself. The whole world being hier-archically structured, inequality applies to all living creatures as well as

145 Ibid., p. 242.
146 Ibid., vol. I, p. 241.
147 Ibid., vol. II, p. 398.
148 Ibid., p. 363.

to individuals: that is the aristocratic vision of the world advocated by Nietzsche, as well as his notion of superiority and "race," a species of isolated higher men, in opposition to the racist or nationalist notion which considers that entire races or nations are "superior" to others.

Nietzschean elitism has little to do with biological racism and nothing to do with nationalism, the master "race" not being a race in the traditional sense of the word, but a "coming" race of isolated solitaries, aristocrats without a title, a distinct higher species which must prepare the advent of the Superman; as we have already cited, Nietzsche tells us of a "new race," a "new caste of masters" which should be *individually* selected, and not an already existing race or class which is considered *collectively* (we find in this latter case, according to Nietzsche, the same herd instinct as that of the liberals and socialists).

Nietzsche speaks of a "race" mainly in the philosophical and spiritual sense; to him, the words "race" and "caste" are interchangeable. It is not just biological superiority and health but essentially the innate psychic, moral and mental superiority of the individual which should determine his social position. The Brahmanic caste system best illustrates what the German philosopher had in mind when he spoke of the master race as a higher caste.

Indeed, Nietzsche considers that the order of rank exists *within* each race and nation, not *between* races and nations. Castes are in this sense distinct "races" of individuals, different "species" separated from each other by an unbridgeable gulf. Thus, higher men are the "very few" natural aristocrats who could be found in every nation and every race. That explains why Nietzsche despises the nationalist "herd instinct" or what he calls "bovine nationalism," for it claims that the *entire* community or group is "superior" to others, which is untrue and impossible, Nietzsche argues, given the fact that only the isolated exceptional individuals form the universal, transnational aristocracy that he talks and dreams about.

Therefore, Nietzsche's "master race" is a higher caste of exceptional, superior beings belonging to several races and nations; those are the magnificent "blond beasts of prey" possessing the highest degree of mental, moral and psychic strength, vigour and courage, the creators who dominate the vegetating "civilised," peaceful, weak and mediocre masses.

In short, Nietzsche perceives the true superiority of an individual *not just* in *physiological* terms (admitting the existence of "great inequalities at the level of biological capabilities) but also in *degrees of power* of the spirit and character, rather than in social or political terms. He affirms that the difference between men is so great—even within races and nations—that it pushes us to talk of two distinct species: the "masters" and the slaves," two species that have nothing to do with the artificial social hierarchy or national identity.

The famous master race that Nietzsche talks about is thus a supra-national, universal and spiritual concept, transcending races, nations, as well as all homogeneous groups of men. The future lords of the earth will be individuals issued from the elite inside the different races and nations, superior beings who justify on their own existence itself and are consequently destined to form a new people, a new race of masters destined to rule one day over the entire earth.

"Great politics" and the rule of the universal master race

In opposition to the liberal and bourgeois conception of politics, which merely grants the state the basic function of protecting and safeguarding the rights of citizens, Nietzsche introduces his own radically anti-democratic, epic vision of politics, which he names "great politics," a higher politics on an international scale which does not separate the temporal from the spiritual—as does the current secular state—but rather puts the "political" in the service of the "spiritual" (but not the religious, which is for the masses), giving the aristocratic universal government that Nietzsche advocates a sacred mission: that of breeding the future "lords of the earth," the "dominating caste" which reunites "the vastest souls, apt for the most diverse tasks of governing the universe":

> From now on, there will be more favourable conditions for more com-prehensive forms of domination, whose like has never yet existed. And this is not even the most important thing; it is rather the development of the possibility of international species-unions which will set themselves the task of rearing a new master race, the future "lords of the earth";—a vast new aristocracy, based on the most severe self-legislation, in which the will of the philosophical men of power and the artist-tyrants will be given permanence over millennia;—a higher kind of men who, thanks to their superiority in will, riches, and influence, will employ demo-cratic Europe as their most pliant and supple instrument for getting hold of the destinies of the earth, so as to work as artists upon "man"

himself... enough, the time is coming when politics will have a different meaning.[149]

"Great politics" will be different from all that has hitherto been known under the name of politics, for it will bring to power a "new, formidable aristocracy" which will be composed of "despotic philosophers" and "artist-tyrants"; in other words, the master race, the great men, to Nietzsche, have hitherto been beyond politics: "The highest men live beyond the rulers, freed from all bonds, and in the rulers they have their instruments."[150]

Therein lies their greatness, according to Nietzsche, but also their misfortune: "The most unpardonable thing about you: you have the power and you will not rule."[151] Therefore, Nietzsche considers that in order to restore human greatness, the future must necessarily be different; "the highest man" should and shall be "the highest lord," the ruler:

> The best shall rule, the best wants to rule! And where it is otherwise — the best is *lacking*... The highest man should also be the highest lord on earth. There is no harder misfortune in all human destiny than when the powerful of the earth are not also the first men. Then everything becomes false and awry and monstrous.[152]

Justice itself demands that the best also be the first; and so they shall be, Nietzsche asserts: "Behold, I teach you the Superman! The Superman is the meaning of the earth. Let your will say: the Superman *shall* be the meaning of the earth!"[153]

To establish "great politics" or the rule that shall herald the advent of the Superman, Nietzsche underscores the necessity of a conscious and willed determination as well as an organised action; but it is only war, not an aimless war, but the holiest and noblest of wars, the war of the spirit, which shall realise this dream; indeed, history shows that all great events and creations are the product of struggle — even violence — that the higher spirit wages against the lower spirit, a struggle that is both spiritual and real: "A dominating race can grow up only out of terrible

149 Ibid., vol. II, p. 364.
150 Ibid., p. 458.
151 Friedrich Nietzsche, *Thus Spoke Zarathustra*, p. 187.
152 Ibid., pp. 260-261, 299.
153 Ibid., p. 22.

and violent beginnings. Problem: where are the barbarians of the twentieth century?"[154]

These barbarians, who, like Prometheus, "come from the heights," are a "conquering and dominating race which seeks a matter it could mould."[155] The great politics of the future and this "war" will thus be as spiritual as real, given that they will be in the service of the highest and sole truth, that of breeding a new species, the Superman, a cause and a truth which require the complete elimination of all Judeo-Christian values and the "lies of millennia" which form the basis of Western civilisation.

Consequently, when truth "shall step into battle," as Nietzsche says, against these millenarian lies, the whole earth shall tremble and shall be completely transformed beyond what man can imagine. That is when the conception of politics will be "absorbed" by a "war of the spirits" and that all the old structures of society will fly into bits, for they in fact were resting on a lie; that is when the earth will be an arena for spiritual and real wars "as never before"; great politics as prophesied by Nietzsche will thus have unfolded and will accomplish its aim.

To Nietzsche, great politics — i.e. *real* politics; the only politics history retains — is the projection of the will to power on a world scale, the struggle for the domination of the earth by a species of higher men. It is eugenics applied on a universal scale. The concept of "race" according to Nietzsche is in fact, as we have seen, a universal and spiritual concept, transcending the political frontiers of states and nations, as well as the biological determinism of racial theorists; but this "universalism" professed by Nietzsche is in no way a prelude to a universal humanist ideal or a pacifist and liberal internationalism; it is rather an integral trait of his aristocratic vision of the world whose ultimate goal is a world dominated by the master race of distinct character, morality and spirit, which transcends the political, geographical, linguistic and cultural frontiers of nation-states, as well as biological racism.

This supra-statist and supranational Nietzschean philosophy emanates from the very essence of his "selective thought" (which we will study in the next chapter), dominated by the will to create a universal "race" of masters, a distinct species of dominators destined to rule the earth. As we have demonstrated, these "lords of the earth" do not

---

154 Friedrich Nietzsche, *The Will to Power*, vol. II, p. 298.
155 Ibid., p. 338.

exclusively belong to a nation—or a race in the conventional sense of the word—but to the whole earth; consequently, in order to realise their supreme mission, their allegiance must be solely to their race, their species, the master race, and not to the particular nation or culture to which they belong by simple birth, as is the case for vulgar and chauvinistic nationalism:

> O my brothers, I direct and consecrate you to a new nobility; you shall become begetters and cultivators and sowers of the future... O my brothers, your nobility shall not gaze backward, but outward! You shall be fugitives from all fatherlands and fore-fatherlands![156]

In order to face the challenges of the great politics of the future, which will be radically aristocratic and supra-national, the arena of the "wars of the spirit" on a worldwide scale, the members of the master race—these "homeless" lofty souls, separated and dispersed around the globe—should abandon traditional or "narrow" nationalism—"little politics"—in favour of a great aristocratic vision of the world which would serve to unite them and organise them in preparation for their world conquest, as a prelude to the creation of the Superman; thus, the conflict between "masters" and "slaves," between "Supermen" in the making (the "higher men") and the "sub-humans" (or "beast-men") is an international, universal conflict.

Nietzsche calls for a kind of "world aristocratic government" governed by a higher "universal class," a distinct spiritual "race" endowed with physical health and incomparable mental and moral force, a natural nobility of free spirits and higher souls which would prepare the advent of the Superman, heir of God.

---

156 Friedrich Nietzsche, *Thus Spoke Zarathustra*, p. 253.

CHAPTER THREE

Nietzsche's Spiritual Atheism: The Superman, a New Goal for Humanity

Christian morality, which led to the death of the god of Monotheism and produced the "Last Man," incarnated the will to power of the slave; this will pushed the slave to realise a total inversion of values in order to become equal, then "superior" to his ancient pagan masters. As for the Master, *his* will to power pushes him to overcome and vanquish the nihilism that resulted from God's death. By adopting a life-affirmative, heroic, and tragic philosophy, as well as an "immoralism" which restores the natural order of rank, the Master is able to transcend the death of the Christian God, thus paving the way for the birth of a new mode of divinity, incarnated by the Superman, who is the culmination of the process of eternal overcoming inherent in the creative principle of the will to power.

-I- The death of God, or spiritual atheism, prelude to the rebirth of the divine

It is important to reserve a part of this work to what I have called Nietzsche's "spiritual atheism," for it is not an absolute, conventional — that is, materialistic and nihilistic — atheism, hence its unique character and its significant position in Nietzsche's thought. Indeed, the death of God is not, for Nietzsche, the proclamation of an absolute atheist; on the contrary, it constitutes a prelude to the real spiritual rebirth of the divine and its incarnation on earth: the Superman. Nietzsche's atheism is therefore not absolute, yet, as with nihilism, it is a necessary phase of awareness that aims to destroy the old monotheistic god and enable man to experience—and to create—*true* divinity.

But first, one wonders how Friedrich Nietzsche, the first philosopher who had the incredible audacity to proclaim that "God is dead," the iconoclast who philosophised with a hammer, Zarathustra the *Gottlos*, the godless, who spoke thus in his bible: "Who is more godless than I, so I could rejoice in his lesson?"[157] How could this same Nietzsche also speak of the advent of a new God? Moreover, of *which* God did Nietzsche speak when he proclaimed, at the end of *The Will to Power* (his last work that was published posthumously), the advent of a "new mode of divinity" which should and would follow nihilism, this disease so characteristic of modernity, a disease which is at the same time the cause and the logical and inevitable consequence of the death of God?

What at first glance seems contradictory—an "atheist" and a "nihilist" announcing the advent of a new God—can only be explained when we understand that Nietzsche's atheism and nihilism are basically necessary but transitory phases of his "philosophising with a hammer" and not ends in themselves. Nietzsche's atheism and nihilism are indeed an integral part of his thought, whose first step (the "destructive" phase) aims to destroy the old law-tables and to realise a veritable inversion of values, in order to reach the second step of Nietzschean philosophy, the creative phase leading to a higher end, to an act of creation: the Superman. "The goal," Nietzsche affirms in *The Will to Power*, "is *not* mankind but the Superman!"[158]

Thus, to retain from Nietzsche merely the figure of the philosopher who proclaims himself a nihilist and a godless prophet, would be to understand him partially and incompletely, and to disregard his most profound and most significant—and, alas! most ignored—side: his spirituality. Nietzsche's deicide concerns but *one* god (the god of monotheism), and *not* the divine; Nietzsche himself admits this fact in *The Will to Power* in which he says of the refutation of God: "Fundamentally, only the moral God is refuted."[159]

However, it is in *Thus Spoke Zarathustra* that we best grasp the meaning and the essence of Nietzsche's atheism, that we realise what Nietzsche meant by "godless," and we understand why and how Nietzsche could

---

157 Ibid., p. 272.
158 Friedrich Nietzsche, *The Will to Power*, vol. II, p. 418.
159 Ibid., p. 181.

not believe in *this* god precisely because he was a true believer, a believer in his *own* god, a god who affirms life, a god "with light feet," in contrast to the God on the cross; in other words, "Dionysus versus the Crucified."

Indeed, in *Thus Spoke Zarathustra,* the last Pope, put "out of service" by the death of God, explains to the Persian prophet why he came to meet him, "the most pious of all those who do not believe in God"; The Pope adds: "of the two of us I am the most godless!" After having explained to the Pope why he could not believe in such a god, a god of good and evil, a monster of morality, an ambiguous, obscure, heinous, imperfect god, Zarathustra concludes: "Away with such a god! Better no god, better to produce destiny on one's own account, better to be God oneself!" And that is when the Pope pronounces his most surprising response (surprising for a Pope, at least, who has just heard the most blasphemous words): "O Zarathustra, you are more pious than you believe, with such an unbelief! Some god in you has converted you to your godlessness. Is it not your piety itself that no longer allows you to believe in a god?"[160]

We thus understand that if Nietzsche "killed" God (or, more exactly, perceived and proclaimed the death of God, therefore becoming the "gravedigger" of an already dead god), it was out of love, out of pity for the figure of the Crucified that he refused to venerate, for it is a falsified, distorted image of divinity, a symbol of suffering and a morality hostile to life, or the will to decline and to death. Only a true believer in God, a highly spiritual being, could commit such an act, for this god had become an abomination in his eyes, a denial of life.

Seen from this angle, Nietzsche's atheism takes on a totally different significance and becomes a means to reach new levels and new heights of spirituality. Nietzsche rejects the "religious" (which is historical and dogmatic, in contrast to the spiritual, which is eternal and ahistorical) precisely because the superstitious and dogmatic infantilism of religions has destroyed spirituality, that is, real divinity, which is immanent in man and in nature, not outside man and above life.

Nietzsche's spirituality has long been ignored, and scholars have generally only focused on his "destructive" side which was nonetheless but a prelude to his great work of creation, his "creative" and constructive side, his philosophy of eternal self-overcoming which culminates in the advent of the Superman. Nietzsche's atheism is thus only a *means,* a

---

160 Friedrich Nietzsche, *Thus Spoke Zarathustra*, p. 314.

tool that this iconoclast, this "hammer," breaker of idols, uses to liberate humanity from the millenarian lies of the monotheistic god, lies which led to the nihilism of modernity; therefore, his spiritual atheism is an attempt to vanquish and transcend nihilism, a process that Nietzsche, as we have already seen, calls "the self-overcoming of nihilism" or "nihilism vanquished by itself."

-II- The new mode of divinity, a "coming god" beyond good and evil

After having destroyed the idols of religion, Nietzsche advocates a spiritual rebirth and lays the foundations of a new religion, a *Naturreligion* ("religion of nature") and a *Lebensphilosophie* ("philosophy of life") faithful to the real image of divinity, a natural, eternal, universal religion. The old god is dead, long live the new god! In the chapter of *The Will to Power* entitled "the new mode of divinity," Nietzsche writes: "and how many new gods are still possible!", adding: "it is only after the death of religion that the invention of the divine could take all its luxuriance."[161]

Nietzsche, for whom the religious instinct is the creator of gods, thus becomes the prophet of a new form of divinity: "God conceived on the type of creative spirits, the 'higher men,'"[162] and therefore a god accessible to man, a god that symbolises the spirit of the earth.

Therefore, could it thus be that God is *not* dead? Could it be that he is resurrected? Nietzsche answers this question in *The Will to Power*: "You say it is a spontaneous decomposition of God, but he is only shedding his skin: he is casting off his moral epidermis. And soon you shall see him—beyond good and evil."[163]

To Nietzsche, gods too die—and are reborn—like men, for otherwise what would there be to create if gods existed? The will to power is essentially a will to self-overcoming, the will to create—and recreate—gods. Therefore, God shall be reborn in a new form, in conformity with the Nietzschean (Dionysian) principle of eternal recurrence and eternal creation. Nietzsche thus becomes the prophet of the post-Christian and post-liberal era by announcing his rejection of both

---

161 Friedrich Nietzsche, *The Will to Power*, vol. II, p. 454.
162 Ibid., p. 454.
163 Ibid., p. 393.

transcendentalism and materialism, and by prophesising the advent of a "new form of divinity."

Now what are the attributes of such a new form of the divine? This new mode of divinity, this "coming" god that Nietzsche talks about, and consequently the (Dionysian) religion of the future which should replace Christianity following the death of the god of monotheism, will be, first, and without doubt, a pagan god, a God that affirms the great "yes" to all things.[164]

We have already spoken of Nietzsche's spirituality, now we should demonstrate that this spirituality is essentially of pagan inspiration, that is, polytheistic, aristocratic, perfectionist and unitarian (or monistic), a religion of nature, that is, eternal and universal; and, more importantly, Nietzsche being faithful to the "spirit of the earth," the new religion will be an immanentist, pantheistic religion which distinguishes itself from Christianity by not offering an "afterlife" in the skies but instead proposes to elevate man to the divine rank in the here and now, rendering perfection possible in this life.

Nietzsche openly proclaims himself pagan and anti-modern when he says:

> Let us look one another in the face. We are Hyperboreans—we know too much how much we live in seclusion. "Neither by land nor by sea shalt thou find the road to the Hyperboreans": Pindar already knew that of us. Beyond the North, beyond the ice, beyond death.[165]

Nietzsche thus expresses the isolation and the solitude of higher spiritual beings in the mediocre and sterile age of modernity, by alluding to Greek mythology which spoke of the Hyperboreans as being "the race that dwells beyond the North wind," in Borea, a highly advanced spiritual centre which is located somewhere in Northern Europe, according to the legend. The Greek god Apollo, according to Greek mythology, represented the hyperborean sun god.

Nietzsche also clearly declares himself pagan in his famous passage in *The Will to Power* (cited earlier) which he qualifies as his "Dionysian world which eternally creates and destroys itself." Also, the following

---

164 "Are pagan all those who say yes to life, those for whom 'God' is the word which expresses the big 'yes' to all things." Friedrich Nietzsche, *Antichrist*, p. 76.

165 Ibid., p. 15.

passage, from the same book, summarises by itself what paganism, which is intimately linked to Nietzsche's notion of the Superman, means to him:

> We few or many who dare again to live in a dismoralised world, we pagans in faith: we are also the first to grasp what a pagan faith is: — to have to imagine higher creatures than man, but beyond good and evil; to have to consider all being higher as also being immoral. We believe in Olympus — and not in the "Crucified."[166]

Nietzsche preaches the pagan ideal "which strengthens life" as the highest ideal, "a form of religion which would restore human pride";[167] he proposes to "start with the 'aesthetic' ideals where the world appears fuller, rounder, more perfect; the pagan ideal where self-affirmation dominates (we give). Superior type: the classical ideal, expression of a happy blossoming of all the principal instincts."[168]

Nietzsche thus proclaims himself the heir of the ancient pagan spiritual and philosophical tradition; he praises Manu, the first legislator whose code represents a "higher, spiritually incomparable work"; he himself admits in *The Will to Power* that "when I consider the world like a divine game beyond good and evil, I have the philosophy of Vedanta and Heraclitus as precursors,"[169] adding: "Man's highest ambition is to unite with what is strongest. That is the origin of Brahmanism, born in the caste of masters."[170]

Thus, it is from Brahmanism and Greek philosophy that Nietzsche draws his inspiration for his new religion which, as we shall later demonstrate, will be essentially Dionysian in spirit and character. Already in *The Birth of Tragedy*, Nietzsche wrote: "Dare now to be tragic men: for ye are to be redeemed! Ye are to accompany the Dionysian festive procession from India to Greece!"[171] Yet it is mostly the Greek ideal which fascinates Nietzsche, the Greeks whom he considered as "the hitherto highest type of man,"[172] the pagan ideal par excellence: "Of all the races

166 Friedrich Nietzsche, *The Will to Power*, vol. II, p. 393.

167 Ibid., vol. I, p. 157.

168 Ibid., p. 429.

169 Ibid., vol. II, p. 464.

170 Ibid., vol. I, p. 157.

171 Friedrich Nietzsche, *The Birth of Tragedy*, p. 152.

172 Friedrich Nietzsche, *The Will to Power*, vol. II, p. 277.

of man, the most accomplished, the most beautiful, the most envied, the most life-affirming, the Greeks...."[173] And: "I consider Greek morality as the highest that has ever been."[174]

Indeed, Nietzsche considers that perfection resides in the union of Apollo and Dionysus, the former symbolising harmony, order, and reason, the latter eternal becoming, the creative affirmation of life. The "coming" god that Nietzsche talks about will thus be a pagan (probably Greek) god, a god "with light legs," a dancing god, that is, a god who affirms life, who urges men to bless life instead of kneeling before an idol; a god who urges men to be like the gods and even to be gods themselves, instead of weak and submissive slaves, in contrast to god the judge, the jealous god, the god of resentment of what Nietzsche calls Judeo-Christian "monotono-theism."

This new pagan god will be, as Nietzsche's Zarathustra, a *Ja-sager*, a great sayer of yes and amen, that is, he will affirm life, *this* life, as eternal, as the only life and the only reality. Nietzsche says in *The Will to Power*:

> The essential question is not to know whether we are satisfied with ourselves, but whether we are satisfied with anything. If we say yes to a single moment, we have thereby said yes not only to ourselves, but to all of existence. For nothing exists for itself, neither in us, nor in things; and if our soul had once vibrated and resonated as a cord of joy, all eternities have collaborated to determine this sole fact—and in that one moment of affirmation, all eternity was welcomed, redeemed, justified, and affirmed.[175]

Nietzsche thus preaches a "Dionysian affirmation of the universe as it is" (and not as it *should* be), a "Dionysian attitude towards existence," and his formula for this is *amor fati* (love of fate). For Nietzsche measures a man thus: "What amount of truth bears a spirit, what amount of truth does he dare? ... error is cowardice... any conquest of knowledge is the result of courage, of toughness towards oneself, of neatness towards oneself."[176] This *amor fati* will enable man to restore the innocence of becoming and to establish, as the ancient pagans, a direct link with the universe, and hence with divinity, for, as Nietzsche affirms, "outside the

173 Friedrich Nietzsche, *The Birth of Tragedy*, p. 34.
174 Friedrich Nietzsche, *The Will to Power*, vol. II, p. 384.
175 Ibid., p. 465.
176 Ibid., pp. 274-275.

whole, there is nothing"; he thus makes no distinction between God and the universe, both being intimately fused in a cosmic whole.

It is therefore a monistic, holistic, pantheistic vision of the universe that Nietzsche offers us, which means the coming God will be a real god, not an imagined god, not a god in heaven, but an immanent god, inherent in nature, in man (at least in the exceptional man). For Nietzsche, there is no duality between the soul and the body, between God and man (the higher man), between this life and the other. He asserts a higher monism, a pantheism that only the masters possess.

It is a new conception of divinity, or rather a return to the ancient pagan conception of religiosity, whose God was accessible to man and whose gods *were* men. However, unlike the pantheists, Nietzsche wants to rehabilitate nature by humanising it, not by divinising it;[177] to "humanise" the universe for Nietzsche is equivalent to "feel ourselves more and more its masters."[178]

When Nietzsche adds that "every individual collaborates to the whole of the cosmic being—consciously or not, willingly or not," he espouses an immanent conception of the divine, which transcends the "I" and the "You" in order to "feel in a cosmic way."[179] Nietzsche rejects the "Kingdom of Heaven," infantile fantasy of the weak and the cowardly, to venerate only the "Kingdom of Earth," a world that is much richer, more real, reserved to virile and complete men; he opposes the divine, which is immanent and polytheistic, that is, the creator of gods, to monotheism's transcendent god.

Thus, the new god will not be a god for all; he will be a hierarchical god, for it is each one's religiosity which determines which god he will have; in other words, each has his own god, each deserves his own god, according to his degree of spiritual elevation. That is what Nietzsche calls the "great selective thought," the hierarchy of thoughts and types of men:

> We need a doctrine strong enough to exert a selective action: strengthening the strong, paralysing and breaking those who are weary of life... my philosophy brings the triumphant thought which shall finally destroy all other ways of thinking. It is a great selective thought: the races that could not bear it are condemned; those who shall feel it as the

177 Ibid., p. 453.
178 Ibid., p. 460.
179 Ibid., p. 460.

supreme good are chosen to dominate... the same circumstances that cause the weakening of man elevate into greatness the stronger and rarer souls,.. the circumstances which will enable a *strong* and *higher* species to subsist (I mean in the matter of spiritual discipline) are the opposite of those that are necessary to the industrial masses, to the mercantile masses that Spencer speaks of. That which is desirable only to *the strongest* and *most fertile* natures, for that facilitates their existence—leisure, adventure, incredulity, the very excesses—would necessarily ruin the mediocre natures if they had access to them; and it is in fact that which ruins them. That which befits those, is the assiduity at work, the rule, temperance, firm "conviction," in short the "virtues of the herd"; it is they who bring this humanity to its perfection.[180]

Men being unequal, there are consequently two kinds of morality but also two kinds of religiosity, two kinds of gods: the god of masters and the god of slaves. Whereas the Judeo-Christian god was the god of slaves, Nietzsche's coming god will be the god of masters. To Nietzsche, the master, the strong man, whose ego "wants to beget his god and put mankind on its knees before this god," creates his own god, an immanent god, in his image, whereas the slave kneels before a god that will forever remain a stranger to him, forever unreachable, a transcendent god born from fear and weakness.

These two antithetical gods will always be in conflict, so long as men shall live: "Divine man creates his own God; and there is no worse enmity on earth than the enmity between gods."[181] The Nietzschean God will be in the image of Greek gods, who are neither totally gods, nor totally men, rather god-men; he praises the Greeks for not having known "that gap between divine beauty and human ugliness."[182]

This dichotomy between divinities reflects itself also in religions which all have an esoteric, eternal and universal side, reserved for the initiated, and an exoteric, historical, dogmatic side addressed to the masses. The inversion of values advocated by Nietzsche thus implies the inversion of divinities; whereas in the era of the Judeo-Christian God, the slave morality predominated, the era of the Nietzschean God will restore the natural order of rank and thus the supremacy of aristocratic

---

180 Ibid., pp. 110, 340-341, 372.
181 Ibid., p. 434.
182 Ibid., vol. I, p. 156.

values, an aristocracy of the spirit (unlike the conventional hereditary aristocracy based on titles and possessions) of Brahmanic type.

The coming god conceived by Nietzsche will not be the god of goodness or wisdom, but the god of supreme force:

> Let us let the concept of God far from the supreme Good; it is unworthy of a God. Let it also be far from supreme Wisdom: it is the vanity of philosophers which has imagined this absurdity, a God that would be a monster of wisdom: they wanted him to resemble them as much as possible. No! God is supreme Power: that is enough! From this results all things, from this results... the "world."[183]

This Nietzschean God, incarnation of the will to power, of the inexhaustible and creative will to live, will be a god beyond good and evil; for power, creative energy, always expresses itself beyond good and evil. Nietzsche explains in *Ecce Homo* that *his* Zarathustra had corrected the good/evil duality of the historical Zarathustra, a duality which had led to Christianity. The new Zarathustra, alias Nietzsche, is the prophet of a new divinity, a new religion which transcends morality, as power is beyond morality. Nietzsche writes: "If we proceed from experience, from a random case where a man has risen sensibly above the measure of humanity, we will see that all higher degree of power implies freedom towards good and evil, as towards 'true' and 'false.'"[184]

When Nietzsche says that God is shedding his skin and "soon you shall see him—beyond good and evil,"[185] he considers that the supreme good and the supreme evil are identical, as long as they beget creative power.

The coming god will be a god of becoming, the god of eternal recurrence. Nietzsche considers that if the world had an end, that end would have been attained; thus, the world, "even if it is no longer a god, must however possess virtually the divine creative force, a force of infinite metamorphosis... the world, as force, must not be conceived as unlimited, for it cannot be conceived thus; we forbid ourselves the concept of an infinite force because it is incompatible with the concept of 'force.'"[186]

183 Ibid., vol. II, pp. 463-464.
184 Ibid., vol. I, p. 132.
185 Ibid., vol. II, p. 443.
186 Ibid., vol. I, pp. 340-341.

Thus, what may seem as an outright form of nihilism — the eternal recurrence of all things — is in fact a supreme affirmation of life, of this life, the only life, the real life, a creative call to perfection in the here and now (and not in an undefined, illusory "beyond"): "Let us stamp on our own life the seal of eternity! This thought is heavier in content than all religions which despise this life and which have taught us to look towards a badly defined life."[187]

Nietzsche adopts Heraclitus' maxim "everything is in flux," and opposes the pagan immanentist thought of becoming to the Christian transcendental thought of being. The eternal recurrence is to Nietzsche the only remedy to the death of the transcendent God, given that it enables man to determine his own destiny, for eternity. Nietzsche writes: "Live in a way that you would wish to live, it is the duty — for you shall relive, in any case! Eternity depends on it!"[188] It is thus a call to "explain becoming without passing by intentions of finality,"[189] for "if everything is determined, how could I dispose of my acts?"[190]

Nietzsche believes that, "in order to bear the thought of eternal recurrence, one must be free towards morality,"[191] and asks himself: "If we eliminate from evolution the idea of an end, would we nonetheless affirm evolution? Yes, if inside this evolution and during each of its moments an end would be attained, and always the same end."[192] This end, to Nietzsche, is none other than eternal self-overcoming, to finally reach the stage of the Superman, that is, the God-Man, the god in the making, the incarnated god and not the god "in heaven."

This Nietzschean god of becoming will also be the god of eternal self-overcoming, of creative evolution, which represents the law of nature and of life. Indeed, to Nietzsche, life — that is, God himself (given his monistic vision of the universe) — is but an eternal self-domination, an eternal overcoming. Becoming is thus creative, it never ceases to reinvent itself. From a convinced nihilist to an accomplished nihilist (who has vanquished his nihilism by transcending it), Nietzsche shows us the way

187 Ibid., vol. II, pp. 288-289.
188 Ibid., p. 345.
189 Ibid., vol. I, p. 102.
190 Ibid., vol. II, p. 344.
191 Ibid., p. 345.
192 Ibid., p. 13.

to tread in order to give life a new meaning, after the fall of the old moral world.

Refusing to adopt a pessimistic and destructive attitude which makes life denial the only goal (as an escape from the suffering of a vain and futile existence), as Schopenhauer and the Buddhists did before him, Nietzsche, who saw in the will to perfection the "last residue of the divine," chooses by contrast a tragic, heroic attitude towards life, the "pessimism of force," or "active nihilism." He decides to overcome, transcend his nihilism by setting for himself—and for humanity—a new goal: the Superman, apex of becoming and self-overcoming.

However, the law of overcoming implies for man to sacrifice his "human, all-too human" side, to realise a real spiritual mutation of his being. He must consume himself in his own flame to be reborn as a phoenix from his ashes. For the divine in man to be born, the human in him must perish. That is why Nietzsche praises, from the bottom of his heart, in *Thus Spoke Zarathustra*, "those who decline… for they go beyond."[193] The higher man is he who aspires after the divine in full knowledge that, as Icarus, he must perish to attain his goal. Nietzsche writes in his *Zarathustra*: "Always more numerous, always better must those of this kind perish… only thus will man grow to the height where the lightning will strike him and break him, high enough for the lightning."[194]

This man of the heights, of the peaks, this mutant of the spirit who has overcome himself, who has overcome his human condition, is none other than the *Übermensch*, the Superman, the supreme goal and apotheosis of Nietzschean thought.

-III- The Superman, a new goal for humanity

Nietzsche's Superman is the incarnation of this new, "coming" God, of the resurrection of the divine following the death of the monotheistic god. The Superman is the masterpiece and cornerstone of Nietzsche's philosophy; he is at once the culmination of the principle of eternal overcoming, of the will to power, and the supreme goal for humanity. Following the death of God, the only hope for mankind, lost and without ideals, is the incarnation of an immanent divinity, of the divine on earth, the *Übermensch*, man's new accessible goal.

---

193 Friedrich Nietzsche, *Thus Spoke Zarathustra*, p. 249.
194 Ibid., p. 349.

Nietzsche considers that the death of God was necessary in order to create the Superman, for the latter represents, in his eyes, the new mode of divinity. The Superman is thus the incarnation of Nietzsche's coming god whom, as we have seen, is an immanent, pantheistic god. Therefore, to speak of Nietzsche's coming god is ineluctably to speak of his human manifestation, the Superman. We cannot separate, in Nietzsche's philosophy, the concepts of the divine and the Superman, for, according to his monistic vision of the world and of divinity, they are inseparable and of the same nature: the Superman is a God-Man, and thus a god in the making, a "coming god."

As we have seen, the "death of God," to Nietzsche, far from representing the destructive and absolute nihilism of an absolute materialist, is rather a profoundly spiritual event, announced by a true believer in human perfection; indeed, it is only by repudiating the existence of a transcendent god and the promise of perfection in the "beyond," that the higher man could be resuscitated as lord and master of the earth, as a Superman, a God-Man who symbolises terrestrial perfection and the new and highest—but realisable—goal of mankind, for man cannot bear life without giving it a meaning; mankind cannot live without a goal, for "if an end is still lacking for humanity, is not what is still lacking—humanity?" asks Nietzsche.[195]

The new goal for mankind, the only hope to vanquish and transcend nihilism, is the divine man, the man who is a god, the god who is a man: "God died, now we desire that the Superman shall live… to you, higher men, this god was your greatest danger" affirms Nietzsche in his bible, *Thus Spoke Zarathustra*.[196]

By calling for the creation of a higher humanity, Nietzsche thus becomes the prophet of the Superman as the "meaning of the earth," the projection of the will to power, a "humanly conceivable, humanly visible, humanly attainable" goal—which can and must realise itself through man's creative will—and not an imaginary supposition: "God is a supposition… could you create a god? Could you conceive a god?—So be silent about all gods! But you could surely create the Superman… once you said 'God' when you gazed upon distant seas; but now I have taught

195 Ibid., p. 81.
196 Ibid., p. 347.

you to say 'Superman'... the beauty of the Superman came to me as a shadow. Ah, my brothers! What are the gods to me now!"[197]

As we have already demonstrated, eternal self-overcoming represents in Nietzsche's eyes the noblest manifestation of the will to power; this creative process culminates in the creation of the Superman: "*Ich lehre euch den Übermensch*" ("I teach you the Superman"), writes Nietzsche in his *Zarathustra*, he who walks among men as among fragments of men, searching for the representative of the new humanity. "I write for a species of man that does not yet exist, for the 'masters of the earth,'" he tells us in *The Will to Power*.[198]

What Nietzsche means by "noontide and eternity" in his *Zarathustra* is the advent of the *Übermensch* who returns eternally to perfect humanity (the Superman incarnates the "noontide," the apex of Nietzschean thought, for all eternity). Zarathustra proclaims: "Dead are all the gods: now we want the Superman to live!—let this be one day, at the great noontide, our ultimate will,"[199] for, Nietzsche pursues: "That precisely is godliness, that there are gods but no God!"[200]

To Nietzsche, the Superman must rule the earth, for he represents the future of the human race, a higher species of man: he is the purest, the strongest, he is perfection itself, he embodies the union between the Apollonian and the Dionysian principles and visions of the world. The Superman is the synthetic man, the artist philosopher, the great legislator of the future, "the union of the creator, the lover, the seeker, in power... the great synthesis of the creator, the lover, the destroyer."[201] He is a Friedrich Nietzsche, the great reformist of humanity who "imposes his hand over the coming millennium" for he is "this predestined man who sets values for millennia."[202]

In *The Will to Power*, his last, unpublished work, Nietzsche predicts how the Superman shall speak: "I have for the first time united in myself the just, the hero, the poet, the savant, the soothsayer, the leader; I have extended my vault over the peoples, I have built columns over which a sky stands—strong enough to carry a sky."[203]

197 Ibid., pp. 110-111.
198 Friedrich Nietzsche, *The Will to Power*, vol. II, p. 442.
199 Friedrich Nietzsche, *Thus Spoke Zarathustra*, p. 104.
200 Ibid., p. 252.
201 Friedrich Nietzsche, *The Will to Power*, vol. I, p. 7.
202 Ibid., vol. II, p. 450.
203 Ibid., p. 457.

The Superman, exact antithesis to modernity's "last man," represents the zenith of the aristocratic vision of the world, incarnating values that are totally different from those of ordinary humans, from the common and the mediocre. This radically elitist concept of Superman only applies to beings of exception, it is even a species "that is yet unborn," as Nietzsche says; indeed, self-overcoming, and consequently the creation of the Superman, is a goal reserved to the rare higher and creative spirits, and remains an impossible dream for common mortals who, according to Nietzsche, have no inherent value. Nietzsche indeed distinguishes between the "superfluous," the "many too many" and the very few "solitaries," the natural aristocrats.

Thus, it is only by dedicating itself to the creation of a higher type that humanity could one day give a meaning to life, the goal being "not mankind but the Superman." The Superman is thus the only, highest goal that mankind could attain and create, the living incarnation and culmination of the will to power.

Self-overcoming includes self-mastery; man must be the master and not the slave of his passions, the latter being merely a means to attain greatness, not an end in themselves. But self-overcoming, for Nietzsche, transcends mere self-mastery to mean the spiritual overcoming of man's "human, all-too-human" condition, that is, the creation of "something beyond man": the Superman, the man who resembles—and is equal to—the gods. The Superman is thus much more than the man who has overcome his passions, he is the man who has transcended his human nature and has become "something more than man."

The creation of the Superman is thus a quasi-impossible mission reserved for the very rare higher beings, for it implies self-mastery and a Spartan or stoic hardness towards oneself as well as towards others: "Praise to what makes hard!" says Nietzsche, adding: "I do not praise the land where butter and honey—flow!"[204] But most importantly, self-overcoming requires a readiness and a willingness—even a strong desire—to suffer and to sacrifice oneself for the sake of the sacred cause of the creation of a higher humanity, and herein lies the real test of greatness for Nietzsche:

> I love those... who sacrifice themselves to the earth, that the earth may one day belong to the Superman... I love him who wants to create beyond

---

204 Friedrich Nietzsche, *Thus Spoke Zarathustra*, p. 192.

himself, and thus perishes...[205] O creators! You must now momentarily live in the world! You would *nearly* perish—and then you will bless this labyrinth where you were lost. Otherwise you wouldn't be able to create, but only to *decline*. You must have your dawns and your twilights. You must have your pains and bear them for a while. You who shall return eternally, you yourselves must become an eternal cycle.[206]

It is only by "declining" that man creates above and beyond himself. Those who make history are the superior and distinguished characters with lofty ideals, those who are ready to sacrifice themselves for these noble ideals. What Nietzsche means by "self-overcoming" thus goes well beyond self-mastery; this spiritual and creative process implies—and culminates in—the creation of the Superman as the "meaning of the earth."

In contrast to God, the Superman is a goal that one can conceive, attain, create. Thus Nietzsche concludes that "maybe man will not stop rising the day he ceases to flow into God."[207] The Nietzschean Superman is thus the manifestation of God on earth, of the new mode of divinity, of the "coming" God, in conformity with the Nietzschean monistic and holistic vision of God as immanent in the world, in nature, in life, and thus accessible to man, even manifested *in* man; in other words, the Superman is the God-Man, the man who has invented God, the man who, like Prometheus, has *become* a god. The following passage illustrates the Nietzschean conception of the God-Man:

> Did Prometheus first have to *imagine* having *stolen* light and pay for it before he could finally discover that he had created light by *desiring* light, and that not only man but also god was the work of *his own* hands and had been clay in his hands? All mere images of the sculptor—no less than delusion, theft, the Caucasus, the vulture, and the whole tragic *Prometheia* of those who know?[208]

Thus, to Nietzsche, it is man who creates God; the religious sentiment consists in creating gods: "The only positive form of religious sentiment has turned in me into love of my ideal, it has become creative: only

205 Friedrich Nietzsche, *Thus Spoke Zarathustra*, pp. 24, 86.
206 Friedrich Nietzsche, *The Will to Power*, vol. II, p. 431.
207 Friedrich Nietzsche, *The Gay Science*, p. 224.
208 Ibid., p. 238.

god-men."[209] It is the act of creation itself, the creative will that is divine, for, as Nietzsche asks himself. "If gods existed, how could I endure not to be a god? Therefore, there are no gods."[210] He continues: "What would there be to create if gods—existed?"[211] The Superman is thus the man who has reinvented himself as a human god, the man who has become a god, thanks to his creative will; therein lies his superiority to God, a superiority that Nietzsche does not fail to underscore in *Zarathustra*: "The beauty of the Superman came to me as a shadow. O my brothers, what are the gods to me now?"[212]

The Nietzschean conception of the Superman is an elevation, it enables man to reach divine aesthetic states, it elevates man to god, in contrast to the Judeo-Christian conception of man as fallen from his divinity because of the original sin, which remains a curse that haunts and plagues man throughout his existence. The concept of Superman represents the union between the body and the spirit, it is neither transcendental nor materialistic; rather, it is transcendence (the overcoming of man) in immanence (the God-Man, a reachable goal).

-IV- Dionysus reincarnated: A promise of noontide and eternity

Who then is this pagan god who incarnates the affirmation of life, this immanent god, this aristocratic god, this god of force who manifests himself beyond good and evil, this god of becoming, of perpetual overcoming, of eternal recurrence, of eternal creation and destruction? Are not these attributes of Nietzsche's "coming" God—and Superman—the same attributes as those of Dionysus, the Greek god of passion, frenzy and intoxication, the god conceived from the type of superior spirits, of higher men,[213] this human and superhuman "dancing god"? The passage already cited in this book, in which Nietzsche describes the "world" as his "Dionysian universe," firmly confirms this hypothesis.

Dionysus, the god who saved reason from nihilism, the god of becoming, of the supra-rational, of the irrational, of the will to power, of

---

209 Friedrich Nietzsche, *The Will to Power*, vol. II, p. 455.
210 Friedrich Nietzsche, *Thus Spoke Zarathustra*, p. 111.
211 Ibid., p. 112.
212 Ibid., p. 113.
213 Friedrich Nietzsche, *The Will to Power*, vol. II, p. 454.

perpetual creation and destruction, is indeed the "new mode of divinity," the incarnated god, the God-Man whom Nietzsche was extolling in his writings. Since his youth, Nietzsche has venerated this god, proclaiming himself his disciple throughout his life, to end up by completely identifying himself with him towards the end of his life: indeed, he signs as Dionysus his latest work, *"Dithyrambs of Dionysus,"* an anthology of philosophical poems. Moreover, Nietzsche chooses the name "Dionysus Philosophos" for the last chapter of his posthumous writings published under the title *The Will to Power*. In this chapter, he reveals the mystical link which binds him since his youth to this god: "In my youth I encountered a dangerous divinity and I cannot tell anyone what had then swept my soul, in evil as in good."[214]

Already, in *Twilight of the Idols*, Nietzsche described himself as "the last disciple of the philosopher Dionysus,"[215] and baptised his faith, "the highest of all possible faiths" with the name Dionysus.[216] Dionysus thus represents the Superman, the dancing god, herald of a life-affirming religion and philosophy. Nietzsche adds in *Beyond Good and Evil*:

> The genius of the heart, as this great Hidden possesses, the tempter god, the born flute player, stealer of consciousnesses, whose voice knows how to descend into the depths of the soul... the god Dionysus, the great ambiguous and tempter god, for whom, as you know, I hitherto consecrated my beginnings, in great secret and veneration—I the last disciple of Dionysus and his last initiate.[217]

Zarathustra (alias Nietzsche) was without doubt the prophet of this god, the messenger of the new Dionysian religion; indeed, Nietzsche's Zarathustra represents "the end of the longest error" (that is, the duality between good and evil, between the real world and the imaginary world), he is the precursor of the new mode of divinity, but not divinity itself.

It is in *The Birth of Tragedy* that Nietzsche interprets in a detailed manner the myth of Dionysus, whose dismemberment symbolises the pains of individuation, and whose rebirth represents the end of individuation,

---

214 Friedrich Nietzsche, *The Will to Power*, vol. II, p. 438.
215 Friedrich Nietzsche, *Twilight of the Idols*, p. 102.
216 Ibid., p. 94.
217 Friedrich Nietzsche, *Beyond Good and Evil*, pp. 243-244.

man's re-conquered unity with himself and with nature.[218] Dionysus represents the primordial One—*das Ur-Eine*—which is opposed to Apollo's principle of individuation. However, despite the fact that Dionysus *appears* to be opposed to Apollo (Dionysus represents the irrational, chaos, passion, Apollo represents order and reason), this god is in fact the collective unconscious, "Apollo's underground," he "reveals" himself in Apollo.[219] The reconciliation of these two divinities is to Nietzsche the most important moment of the history of the Greek cult.

Dionysus is thus the god who permits total fusion with nature, with the divine. He represents supreme unity. To Nietzsche, "the word Dionysian expresses the need for unity, everything that surpasses personality, daily reality, society, the abyss of the ephemeral... an ecstatic affirmation of existence in its totality... the great pantheist participation to all joy and all pain... the eternal will to beget, to bear fruit, to be born; the feeling of necessary union between creation and destruction."[220]

Everything leads us to believe that Nietzsche saw in Dionysus the "coming god," the resuscitated god, the god who would be born again "beyond good and evil," after having shed his moral skin. Indeed, does not Dio-nysus mean the "twice born"? This pagan god, at once Greek and foreigner, at once Greek and universal (he symbolises vital force itself) is a god whose universal spirituality links East and West in this "Dionysian festive procession from India to Greece" that Nietzsche praises (let us not forget that Greece has inherited, and has been inspired by, Indian spirituality).

Dionysian intoxication, which represents an ecstasy, "a symbolic intoxication of the highest spirituality" that enables man to pass from the human to the divine, where man "feels his whole being as a divinised form and justification of nature by itself"[221] — this Dionysian intoxication, is it not the supreme form of spiritual elevation? Does it not represent the process of divinisation of man that Nietzsche talks about when he affirms that "when man has perfectly identified himself with mankind, he moves all of nature"?[222] Dionysus is thus undoubtedly and unequivocally Nietzsche's "coming god."

---

218 Friedrich Nietzsche, *The Birth of Tragedy*, p. 94
219 Ibid., pp. 51-52.
220 Friedrich Nietzsche, *The Will to Power*, vol. II, pp. 445-460.
221 Ibid., p. 445.
222 Ibid., p. 446.

Moreover, Nietzsche describes Dionysus as the "joy of a force which begets and destroys, like a perpetual creation."[223] Dionysus is thus the god in the making, the god of eternal recurrence and eternal overcoming who manifests himself in the creative will to power. This leads us to believe that it is Dionysus himself who will be reborn again, albeit in a new form, in conformity with the Nietzschean principle of eternal self-overcoming and the eternally changing nature of Dionysus, this Greek god of becoming.

Finally, Dionysus is the god who incarnates unity, the "exalted affirmation," the "great pantheistic participation" in life:

> The word "Dionysian" expresses the need for unity, everything that transcends personality, daily reality, society, reality, the abyss of the ephemeral; a feeling which passionately, painfully grows and overflows, and expands into darker, fuller, more floating states; an exalted affirmation of life in its totality, always equal to itself through all the changes, equally powerful, equally joyful; the great pantheistic participation to all joy and all pain, which accepts even the most terrible qualities and the contradictions of existence and considers them as sacred; the eternal will to beget, to bear fruit, to be born; the feeling of necessary union between creation and destruction.[224]

Dionysus symbolises more than any other divinity the pagan, tragic cult, that is, the affirmation of life, of force, of joy, in contrast to the image of the Crucified who represents the Christian ideal that is nothing but a negation of life, a curse on life; Nietzsche contrasts Dionysus with the Crucified:

> The two types: Dionysus and the Crucified... but are we not omitting one type of religious man, the pagan? Is the pagan cult not a form of thanksgiving and affirmation of life? Must its highest representative not be an apology for and deification of life? The type of a well-constituted and ecstatically overflowing spirit! The type of a spirit that takes into itself and redeems the contradictions and questionable aspects of existence! It is here I set the Dionysus of the Greeks: the religious affirmation of life, life whole and not denied or in part... Dionysus versus the "Crucified": there you have the antithesis... It is not a difference in regard to their martyrdom- it is in the meaning of it. Life itself, its

---

223 Ibid., p. 644.
224 Ibid., p. 440.

eternal fruitfulness and recurrence, creates torment, destruction, the will to annihilation. In the other case, suffering—the "Crucified as the innocent one"—counts as an objection to this life, as a formula for its condemnation... The god on the cross is a curse on life, a signpost to seek redemption from life; Dionysus cut to pieces is a promise of life: it will be eternally reborn and return again from destruction.[225]

Dionysus is thus Nietzsche's coming god, for he is the god of becoming who incarnates in avatars and reinvents himself perpetually. He is at once a god of the distant past, from a golden age where man lived in perfect communion with nature, and a god of the distant future, an age where man is called upon to elevate himself to the divine rank. It is therefore not a reactionary return to a dead past—or to a dead form of divinity—that Nietzsche advocates, but rather a new manifestation of this god in eternal mutation.

Indeed, Nietzsche insists on the fact that Dionysus represents the god of eternal becoming and consequently must himself return eternally, but under ever new forms, ever higher forms; we must therefore be inspired by the Greeks—and Dionysus is *the* Greek god par excellence—in order to create again, but we should not copy the Greeks, for this is neither desirable nor creative:

> One recognises the superiority of the Greek man, of renaissance man, but one wants to copy it without reproducing the causes or the conditions of existence... a civilisation which runs after that of the Greeks can produce nothing. Without doubt the creative genius can find everywhere to borrow and nourish itself. And that is how we cannot take anything from the Greeks unless we are creators.[226]

Therefore, Nietzsche does not advocate a return to the "primitive past": rather, he says that man is something that should be overcome—even if it is through education, social Darwinism or wars; here we find a teleology and a "transcendence in immanence" (embodied by the Superman), as well as a promise of noontide and eternity. Dionysus is the sign of that which has not yet come, that which has not yet become in man; he is the god of fermentation, but that which "seeks the wine and calls the light."

---

225 Ibid., p. 445.
226 Ibid., pp. 412-413.

CONCLUSION

The Redemption of the Divine

This book's aim was to demonstrate that Friedrich Nietzsche, far from being the absolute nihilist and atheist as he is generally perceived nowadays, was on the contrary a great affirmer of life whose philosophy was imbued with a deep spirituality that motivated and characterised his pantheistic vision of life, revealing itself even in his most violent and most destructive writings. It is true that Nietzsche was, in his own words, "the most ungodly of the godless," but his godlessness, which is so characteristic of him, was itself a justified reaction of a highly spiritual being who refused to believe in a "God" who represented the antithesis to life and nature.

That is why Nietzsche celebrated the death of this life-denying God, as well as the demise of the morality which perpetuated that tyrant-god "above the clouds," for this death of a false god was to him a prelude to the birth—or rather to the rebirth—of the divine, of real divinity which was intimately linked to man, and not an idol fixed in a "beyond" denying all reality and all human greatness. Man, for Nietzsche, must aspire to divinity not by kneeling before an idol that will remain forever unknown and unreachable, but by overcoming himself and by creating "beyond man": by creating the Superman, incarnation of the mystical union between man and God, a union and a link that monotheism had severed through its transcendent and moral vision of a God "in heaven."

Nietzsche thus had his own vision of divinity, a "coming" god who, like Dionysus, would be the god of eternal overcoming (and would thus manifest himself through several incarnations), a god who would be beyond good and evil, beyond Christian life-denying morality.

The goal of this work was to underscore the mystical side of Nietzschean thought, which is unfortunately nearly totally ignored nowadays by both most of his disciples and scholars as well as his adversaries, who—omitting rare exceptions—read him in a superficial way and consequently do not perceive his spiritual and creative side, focusing only on his "destructive" side which they consider as being an end in itself for Nietzsche, whereas it was in fact only a necessary but transitory stage which served his great work of creation: the Superman.

Indeed, Nietzsche was an iconoclast, a breaker of idols, of fixed dogmas hostile to life and to man's elevation, the first free spirit who welcomed the "death of God" (which he was the first to notice) not based on an absolute, nihilistic and materialistic atheism, but as the death of the false god, of monotheism's moral god, seeing in this divine death not an end in itself (which would represent a perpetual nihilism), but rather a prelude to the rebirth of the divine, after having shed its "moral epidermis." The nihilism which Nietzsche perceived and fought against (using it against itself in order to overcome it), was merely a work of destruction in order to rebuild, reinvent a new and authentic divinity incarnated by the Superman, and not the god on the cross which is a counter-nature and a curse wrought on life and on man.

In this sense, the "death of God" represented at the same time the culmination and the end of nihilism (at least for the higher man), given that it permitted the rebirth of an immanent "new mode of divinity" beyond good and evil, in contrast to the moral and transcendent god of Judeo-Christian monotheism. It was thus his own faith which pushed—even forced—Nietzsche to become an atheist, that is, in this case, to reject the abomination, the moral monster that men call "God," who in fact is but a caricature of real divinity, a negation of life, a betrayal of the authentic God which is immanent in nature and in man.

Nietzsche was thus an "atheist" *precisely because* he believed in the divine, that is, the real God. His atheism was not an end in itself, as is the case for the modern positivists and other sceptics and pessimists. The death of God is itself a spiritual event, a creator of new gods and new law-tables which affirm life; it is thus a death which heralds a spiritual rebirth in a deeply Dionysian sense.

It is indeed more than necessary to reveal this mystical aspect and dimension as well as the fundamentally spiritual and creative character of this great philosopher, the "great sayer of yes and Amen," this anti-Christian atheist (for he is a true believer in life and in the god that is an integral part of it, and not in monotheism, which represents a brutal break of the sacred link between man and God). The nihilistic, atheistic, immoral, and destructive side of Nietzsche was thus not an end in itself, but a transitory phase which was necessary to vanquish and transcend the Judeo-Christian values which themselves had led to nihilism and the spiritual decay of mankind.

Nihilism, an evil so characteristic of modernity, was at the same time the cause and the consequence of the death of God, but Nietzsche's "spiritual atheism" transformed this spiritual darkness into a dawn heralding a new form of divinity incarnated by the Superman. The death of God was thus the consequence and culmination of nihilism, but also and essentially the end of the "longest error," that is, life-denying Christian morality which, by making the world a fable through the invention of an imaginary beyond, had undertaken a veritable inversion of life-affirming values, leading to the absence of any goal justifying human existence.

For the pessimists and the modern positivists, this nihilism and this atheism constituted an end, and thus led to a second nihilism, to the perpetuation of nihilism; indeed, modernity offers no viable (philosophical, spiritual) alternative to the death of God, given that it cannot fill the spiritual chasm left by God's demise, the absence of all justification of life, and constitutes a perpetuation of decadence and slave morality (Christianity), through liberalism, its secularised version.

The slave's will to power, which had inverted the ancient pagan values of the masters, therefore only perpetuates nihilism. As for the master, he is pushed by his will to power to transform the death of God into an inversion of values that are hostile to life and of Christianity's millenarian lies, refusing and rejecting nihilism represented by the transcendent and moral God of monotheism.

In order to transcend nihilism and the death of God, the higher man, who represents an elevated degree of moral and psychic power, and thus incarnates a tragic, heroic and life-affirming vision of the world, uses this vital principle (the will to power) inherent in life, this morality beyond good and evil, as eternal overcoming, as an "active nihilism" (or the "pessimism of strength"), as "immoralism" to reestablish the natural order of rank and real divinity, supreme manifestation of the will to power, and not the "Crucified," the god on the cross of the weak and the weary slaves.

The Superman thus becomes the new goal of life, the representative of the "Coming God," incarnated to perfection by the god Dionysus, who represents the religious affirmation of life.

Bibliography

Friedrich Nietzsche, *Ainsi Parlait Zarathustra* (*Thus Spoke Zarathustra*), Paris: Gallimard, 1971.

Friedrich Nietzsche, *Ainsi Parlait Zarathustra* (*Thus Spoke Zarathustra*), Paris: Librairie Générale Française, 1972.

Friedrich Nietzsche, *L'Antéchrist, Ecce Homo* (*Antichrist, Ecce Homo*), Paris: Gallimard, 1974.

Friedrich Nietzsche, *Crépuscule des Idoles* (*Twilight of the Idols*), Paris: Gallimard, 1974.

Friedrich Nietzsche, *Le Gai Savoir* (*The Gay Science*), Paris: Gallimard, 1950.

Friedrich Nietzsche, *La Généalogie de la Morale* (*The Genealogy of Morals*), Paris: Gallimard, 1971).

Friedrich Nietzsche, *Humain, trop Humain* (*Human, all-too Human*), Paris: Librairie Générale Française, 1995.

Friedrich Nietzsche, *La Naissance de la Tragédie* (*The Birth of Tragedy*), Paris: Librairie Générale Française, 1994.

Friedrich Nietzsche, *Par-delà Bien et Mal* (*Beyond Good and Evil*), Paris: Gallimard, 1971.

Friedrich Nietzsche, *La Volonté de Puissance* (*The Will to Power*), vol. I & II, Paris: Gallimard, 1995.

Other titles published by Arktos:

Beyond Human Rights
by Alain de Benoist

Carl Schmitt Today
by Alain de Benoist

Manifesto for a European Renaissance
by Alain de Benoist & Charles Champetier

The Problem of Democracy
by Alain de Benoist

Germany's Third Empire
by Arthur Moeller van den Bruck

The Arctic Home in the Vedas
by Bal Gangadhar Tilak

Revolution from Above
by Kerry Bolton

The Fourth Political Theory
by Alexander Dugin

Hare Krishna in the Modern World
by Graham Dwyer & Richard J. Cole

Fascism Viewed from the Right
by Julius Evola

Metaphysics of War
by Julius Evola

Notes on the Third Reich
by Julius Evola

The Path of Cinnabar
by Julius Evola

Archeofuturism
by Guillaume Faye

Convergence of Catastrophes
by Guillaume Faye

Why We Fight
by Guillaume Faye

The WASP Question
by Andrew Fraser

War and Democracy
by Paul Gottfried

The Saga of the Aryan Race
by Porus Homi Havewala

Homo Maximus
by Lars Holger Holm

The Owls of Afrasiab
by Lars Holger Holm

De Naturae Natura
by Alexander Jacob

Fighting for the Essence
by Pierre Krebs

Can Life Prevail?
by Pentti Linkola

Guillaume Faye and the Battle of Europe
by Michael O'Meara

New Culture, New Right
by Michael O'Meara

The National Rifle Association and the Media
by Brian Anse Patrick

The Ten Commandments of Propaganda
by Brian Anse Patrick

Morning Crafts
by Tito Perdue

A Handbook of Traditional Living
by Raido

The Agni and the Ecstasy
by Steven J. Rosen

The Jedi in the Lotus
by Steven J. Rosen

It Cannot Be Stormed
by Ernst von Salomon

The Outlaws
by Ernst von Salomon

Tradition & Revolution
by Troy Southgate

Against Democracy and Equality
by Tomislav Sunic

Generation Identity
by Markus Willinger

The Initiate: Journal of Traditional Studies
by David J. Wingfield (ed.)

Printed in Great Britain
by Amazon

54999632R00061